Price Management in Financial
Services

Price Management in Financial Services

Smart Strategies for Growth

GEORG WUEBKER,

JENS BAUMGARTEN,

DIRK SCHMIDT-GALLAS and

MARTIN KODERISCH

GOWER

Published by
Ashgate Publishing Limited
Wey Court East
Union Road
Farnham, Surrey
GU9 7PT England

Ashgate Publishing Company
110 Cherry Street
Suite 3-1
Burlington
VT 05401-3818
USA

Georg Wuebker, Martin Koderisch, Dirk Schmidt-Gallas and Jens Baumgarten have asserted their moral right under the Copyright, Designs and Patents Act, 1988, to be identified as the authors of this work.

British Library Cataloguing in Publication Data
Price management in financial services : smart strategies
  for growth
  1. Financial services industry 2. Pricing
  I. Wuebker, Georg, 1967–
  332

Library of Congress Cataloging-in-Publication Data
Price management in financial services : smart strategies for growth / by Georg Wuebker ... [et al.].
    p. cm.
  Includes index.
  ISBN 978-0-566-08821-6
  1. Financial services industry. 2. Pricing. I. Wuebker, Georg, 1967–

  HG173.P75 2008
  332.1068'8--dc22

2007049171

ISBN-13: 9780566088216

Transferred to Digital Printing in 2012

Printed and bound in Great Britain
by Printondemand-worldwide.com

Contents

List of Figures

List of Tables

Introduction

The term "price management" was coined by Simon and Dolan in their 1997 book *Power Pricing*. Two of the most globally recognized thought leaders in pricing research and advice, the authors described their approach to pricing as follows: "Progressive businesses proactively use pricing as a tool for achieving their goals. These advocates of 'price management' recognize the importance of pricing in determining profit and develop deep pricing competencies to consistently deliver improved profits for their companies."

This book is about applying these principles to the financial services industry. We lay out the fundamentals of pricing in a concise and practical format, show how managers can successfully apply them in practice, and explain why pricing is capable of giving businesses a competitive edge. The book is, to a large extent, based on hundreds of strategic pricing projects conducted by the authors at Simon-Kucher & Partners, the most recognized pricing consultancy in the world. Throughout the book, we provide concrete recommendations for optimal price management.

The reader will be provided with recommendations on: price wars, strategic aspects of pricing, effect of price on sales volume, price optimization, intelligent forms of price differentiation, as well as pricing process and pricing organization. Overall, the aim of the book is to provide an understanding of the effects of price on sales and profits and to demonstrate ways for pricing professionals to use pricing to increase profits.

The book will answer a variety of key management questions, including:

- What are the reasons for the increased importance of pricing in financial services institutions, and how can pricing be used to increase profits?

- Why are pricing principles needed, and how can these be developed?

- How should financial services institutions position themselves in the market with regard to pricing, and what is an appropriate price and product strategy?

- What are the reasons for price wars in the financial services industry, and what strategies can be deployed to avoid price wars?

- What is a price-response function and how can this function be reliably determined to optimize prices for financial services products?

- What is a pricing process and how can a systematic pricing process be developed?

- What effect does brand have on pricing, and vice-versa?

- What intelligent forms of price differentiation exist (e.g. interest rate tiers, added-value account packages, and family prices)?

- What psychological aspects should be taken into account in pricing (e.g. customer perception of interest rates and discounts) and what are their implications for price communication?

- What effect does pricing have on the organization and is there a need for a "Head of Pricing" position in financial services institutions?

- What aspects of price implementation should be considered (e.g. enforcing prices in sales negotiations)?

- How should pricing be monitored by financial services institutions?

- How can the challenges of pricing in different business areas (e.g. B2B, B2C or fund business) and segments (retail, private banking and commercial customers) be solved?

Throughout the book, answers to the above questions are revealed with the help of numerous case study examples.

The book consists of nine chapters.

Setting the scene in Chapter 2, we explore the fundamentals of pricing and why pricing is growing in relevance. We point out the key drivers raising the importance of pricing throughout the financial services industry, and draw particular attention to the damage caused by price wars – common in today's fiercely competitive markets.

- In Chapter 3, we provide the reader with an overview of the fundamental building blocks of pricing and examine how pricing and strategy interact.

- In Chapter 4, we explore price optimization methodologies and use case studies to show how optimization methods have been successfully implemented by financial services organizations around the world.

- In Chapter 5, we go beyond the basic methodologies of price optimization and get to the heart of pricing. Using various case studies, we show how to apply key pricing strategies in the financial services industry, including price differentiation, price bundling, non-linear pricing and multi-person pricing.

- Chapter 6 describes the key psychological aspects of pricing (price awareness, price perception, price image and price thresholds) and shows how financial services organizations can make use of them.

- In Chapter 7, we show how to confront the various obstacles encountered when putting pricing decisions into action. We explore the important question of what a manager should consider when implementing pricing strategies (pricing organization, pricing information systems, price enforcement).

- The case studies in Chapter 8 provide a step-by-step account of pricing in action. We demonstrate how financial services companies have implemented pricing. The pricing methodologies described in the book are at the center of each example.

- The book's final chapter provides managers with an overview of the key learnings from the book.

Fundamentals of Modern Pricing

Increasing relevance of pricing

Many businesses set prices using a combination of instinct, rule of thumb ("we base our prices on our main rival or competitors") and subjective opinion. Financial institutions are no different. This approach to pricing all too often results in lost revenues and strategic mistakes. Headlines describing the consequences of such pricing mishaps are becoming more prevalent: "Direct banks are putting margins under pressure"; "… in times of increasing price sensitivity"; "Bartering at the bank counter"; "Disastrous price wars …". In a research study conducted by Simon and Dolan (1997), 187 executives in Europe and USA, including financial services managers, were asked about the areas of marketing in which they experienced the most competitive pressure and faced the greatest problems. The results placed pricing at the top of the list.

Price is not only important from the competitor perspective. A wide variety of market studies support the notion that price is increasingly becoming a key customer requirement in financial services. The depersonalization of financial services through online and tele-banking channels partially explains this trend. Customers require fewer of the institution's resources and expect prices to reflect this fact. This presents significant challenges in the pricing of financial services products. The key drivers that have led to a change in the landscape of the financial services industry and a greater reliance on price management are set out in the following section.

INTERNET-ENABLED PRICE TRANSPARENCY AND COMPARABILITY

In 2008, the percentage of US households with Internet access hit 70 percent. This percentage will continue to rise as will the level of mobile phone penetration. Recent studies report that around two thirds of all Internet users compare prices online. The importance of online banking is similarly increasing, and this trend is occurring around the world. Approximately 47 percent of EU citizens use the Internet regularly (at least once a week at home or at work). In Germany, the number of online accounts has increased from 3.8 million in 1998 to over 35 million today.

The proliferation of Internet usage across the world has allowed suppliers to reduce costs and pass savings onto customers. Checking accounts that actually pay customers a monthly incentive to use online services have sprung up in the market. In the US, the aggressive pricing of online brokerages such as Charles Schwab and TD Ameritrade has forced traditional banks such as Bank of America to continuously decrease prices and to even offer selected customer segments free trades.

INCREASING REGULATORY REQUIREMENTS

Around the globe, regulatory authorities are increasing their influence on the pricing of financial services products. Since 2003, the Swiss Investment Fund Association (SFA) has required its members to include a "Total Expense Ratio" (TER) in any investment fund price quote. In doing so, the SFA, together with the Swiss Stock Exchange, has attempted to bring transparency to the fund market. As a result, more than 90 percent of all authorized investment funds now provide a TER. Providers like e-fundresearch.com regularly calculate the average TER for various fund types in Switzerland. This level of transparency clearly increases price pressure for those providers whose services are more expensive than the published benchmark.

In the UK, the Office of Fair Trading (OFT) has increased its level of intervention in the UK financial services market. In order to limit the penalty that credit card issuers can charge customers on late payment of monthly interest charges, it has placed a ceiling on late payment fees. Similar intervention is expected for unauthorized overdraft penalties for checking accounts.

CHANGE IN CUSTOMER BEHAVIOUR

The needs of banking customers change significantly over time. Whereas once customers expected personal service at a bank branch, they now demand high quality electronic banking services. As a consequence, the need for banks to develop personal relationships with customers has become less important. Direct banks and insurers are at the forefront of this market development. In 2008, the number of US households using online banking reached more than 40 million (80 million in Europe). From a customer perspective, the cost savings from a "self-service" online bank far outweigh any lack of personal service. Research suggests that only one in 20 direct customer interactions with a bank employee are for a personal financial consultation. Indeed, around 40 percent of customers surveyed indicated that they would prefer to visit their local bank less often in the future – an alarming trend for incumbent banks with significant branch networks. While this points in the direction of the continued growth of direct banks, incumbent banks must respond by developing value-added products and services supported by innovative pricing (see Chapter 5 for more detail).

UNCERTAIN ECONOMIES LEADING TO HIGHER PRICE AWARENESS

In many developed economies, declining real income and employment market uncertainties have created a culture of increased price awareness. For example, ING Direct has grown in the US from a virtual unknown to a powerhouse with more than 5 million customers and more than $62 billion in assets by positioning its products as "Simple, Quick and Cheap". In Germany, ING DiBa has brought in more than 6.5 million customers and more than €76 billion in total assets with this strategy. ING Direct is currently the world's leading direct savings bank with over 18 million customers worldwide.

NEW COMPETITORS WITH AGGRESSIVE PRICING AND INNOVATIVE OFFERINGS

The range of competition in the market has widened through the advent of new products, innovative and differentiated pricing, as well as more aggressive communication strategies. An ever increasing variety of businesses are competing for the same customers. This growing list includes financial services arms of retail businesses, such as BMW Financial Services (Germany), Marks & Spencer Money and Tesco Personal Finance (UK). Through more aggressive marketing, sales campaigns, and low prices, these new entrants have built up sizable customer bases, winning market share from incumbents.

There has also been an emergence of rewards and loyalty programs. More and more businesses, from retail companies to airlines, have started issuing credit cards with the aim of reducing customer churn and increasing cross-selling opportunities. MBNA Europe Bank (UK) issues credit cards on behalf of popular English football clubs: Chelsea's Rewards Credit Card, the official 5 star Liverpool FC Rewards Credit Card, and the Manchester United Credit Card are all tailored to the clubs' fans and can be linked to customized benefits (e.g. discounted ticket prices).

INCREASING GLOBALIZATION OF BANKS

Globalization has changed the role of international price management in financial services. Merging customer habits and industry standards, lower trade barriers and IT costs, and increasing transparency of information are all driving previously isolated domestic markets together and making price differentiation between regions more difficult. Many financial services providers are venturing out of their domestic markets and entering foreign markets. Financial services institutions such as Citi, Bank of America, the Royal Bank of Scotland Group (RBS) and ING Direct leverage economies of scale to create significant cost advantages over smaller local incumbents. Although unified global pricing scenarios proposed by globalization advocates Steven Levitt or Kenichi Ohmae may be somewhat extreme, it is clear that the pressure on prices, and, with it, the importance of international price management, is increasing (see Chapter 5).

Profit destruction from price wars

When other forms of competitive differentiation are ignored and price becomes the only means of competition, price war situations arise. Price wars are occurring in a variety of global industries, including airline, retail, telecommunications and financial services. This downward price spiral (see Figure 2.1) results in profit and value destruction for all market participants. Numerous examples from various industries can be witnessed:

- Grocery stores have been stuck in a price war for many years. The catalyst has often been the entry of global giants such as Wal-Mart into regional markets.

- Telecommunications companies have also experienced a worldwide drop in prices. Following deregulation, the price of long-distance calls dropped by over 70 percent in most markets. Today, they continue to fall at an annual rate of 10 to 20 percent.

- The automotive industry has experienced particularly fierce price wars between major manufactures such as Ford and General Motors.

- Prices in the airline sector have been knocked down by no frills airlines such as Southwest and easyJet.

As the following examples show, similar price wars are all too evident in the financial services industry.

RETAIL BANKING IN GERMANY

Years ago, Dresdner Bank, Germany's third largest bank, was attempting to defend its retail business against attacks from foreign competitors. The bank

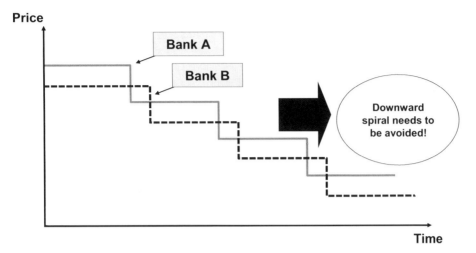

Figure 2.1   Typical financial services price war

created a series of new consumer credit products, sold mainly through Dresdner Cetelem Credit Bank. "Our products will be priced low in order to acquire business from providers such as UK's Royal Bank of Scotland," according to an announcement by the Chairman of the Board, Herbert Walter. This war was a reaction to the growth of foreign providers (e.g. RBS and Santander) in the German market. RBS started to distribute its products through Tchibo, a German retailer, and acquired more than 1.2 million customers in the span of only 2 years, mainly due to the low rates offered on its credit cards. In the battle for the mass market, Dresdner Bank's new sales offensive contributed to the price war and drove prices down even further.

MORTGAGES IN NEW ZEALAND

New Zealand's ASB Bank offered customers discounted fixed rate mortgage products on the TradeMe Internet auction site. For the duration of a 7 day auction, TradeMe members were able to bid on the annual interest rate they were willing to pay on a AU$100,000 ASB mortgage.

MORTGAGES IN SWITZERLAND

Evidence of price wars can also be seen in the Swiss mortgage sector. There, Post Finance, the banking subsidiary of the national postal service, aggressively acquired new business with a discounted fixed term mortgage and even paid the first 6 monthly payments for the customer. Analysis indicated that an increasing portion of new mortgages in the Swiss market included these types of discounts, even if the implied margins often did not fully cover costs.

ONLINE BROKERAGE

Online brokerage services have become particularly price-oriented, resulting in many players exiting the market. Only three of ten online brokers in Switzerland five years ago are still in business today. In the US, the price war in the online brokerage sector recently entered a new phase. Charles Schwab reduced many of its fees and commissions by up to 35 percent, and the stock market reacted negatively to these margin reducing price cuts – following the announcement, share prices in the entire online brokerage sector fell by between 2–3 percent. The fight to win online customers has also intensified in Germany, where Citi increased competition with online and direct banks by aggressively slashing its prices. "We want to unravel the market," a senior manager at Citi said.

RETAIL BANKING IN FRANCE

Competitive price pressure has also started to increase in France. In 2006, the French retail bank Caisse d'Epargne was the first to start paying interest on its checking accounts, something which had at the time only been permitted in France for a year. The move was a sign of greater pricing flexibility and an interest rate offensive that strongly affected the price and product strategies of other institutions in the market.

Also in France, the French post office, La Poste, announced that it was transforming itself into a full service bank. With this announcement, the bank aggressively promoted itself in the market. La Poste posed a significant threat to other providers since it could rely on a network of over 17,000 branches. The business quickly generated almost 30 million banking customers holding 11 million checking accounts. "La Poste is shaking up France's banks," read one newspaper headline. It remains to be seen whether this sleeping giant will choose to start a price war.

PRIVATE BANKING IN THE UNITED KINGDOM

In private banking, the battle to win new customers is fought through individually negotiated discounts. In many cases, this has led to untracked discounting having a significant impact on turnover and margin.

Figure 2.2 shows an example of this kind of situation at a private bank. The tiered line represents the list prices at different volumes that are intended to be enforced by individual relationship mangers. Discounts should only be offered as long as volume increases. Each point represents the actual price' enforced for a specific account (i.e. the individually negotiated discount price).

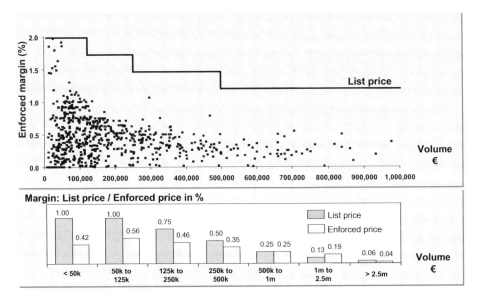

Figure 2.2   Discounts in private banking

The further a point is from the line, the greater the discount the customer received. The result is alarming – just look at the spread of actual prices for any particular volume. Based on our experience, banks often have no transparency of what discounts are actually being given to which customers, and as a result, targeted measures to reduce discounts are often difficult to implement.

WEALTH MANAGEMENT IN THE NETHERLANDS

Increasing customer awareness and a lack of consolidation have not only put significant price pressure on standard banking services' prices and margins, but also on those of wealth management services. To avoid losing unhappy customers, many asset managers are prepared to reimburse part of their management fees. Aiming to prevent customers from switching to another provider, the private banking subsidiary of ABN Amro reimburses part of its management fees if returns do not meet their benchmark.

CORPORATE BANKING IN EUROPE

Large corporate customers are often offered significant discounts. Volkswagen, for example, paid a financing consortium made up of ABN Amro, Citi, Barclays, BNP Paribas, HSBC, and JP Morgan merely 20 basis points above the Euribor rate for a credit facility of €12.5 billion.

FUNDS

With approximately $2 trillion of assets under management, Fidelity Investments is a one of the biggest players in the asset management industry. In the UK, Fidelity offers private investors a range of very low priced investment funds called MoneyBuilder funds. Customers can choose between several different fund types with different equity and fixed income portfolio strategies. MoneyBuilder funds carry a low front-end load and annual management fee, and there are no fees charged for switching between MoneyBuilder funds. The MoneyBuilder funds particularly attract price-conscious customers and new investors.

INSURANCE IN GERMANY

With more than €20 billion in annual premium income, the automotive insurance sector is Germany's third largest sector after life and medical insurance. Auto insurance is considered a key anchor product for selling other policies, therefore the market is highly competitive. A price war had been under way for several years as auto insurers started fighting for customers with aggressive prices in the German insurance market. When a large player, HUK-Coburg, moved up the introduction of its reduced premiums by two months, it was in direct response to the market leader, Allianz, which had previously reduced its premium prices by up to 30 percent in certain target segments. HUK-Coburg, which began as a specialized public sector insurer and rapidly developed into one of Germany's leading discount insurers, introduced its price reductions at just the right time. In Germany, most auto insurance policies can only be cancelled at the end of the calendar year with a 30-day notice period, thus November is the most likely month for customers to switch providers. HUK-Coburg's fast roll out of new premiums was a clear indication of how much Allianz's move affected its business. What was the trigger of this price war? Allianz had started to experience a consistent drop in its business over the past few years, and had lost market share in several core areas. Hence, Allianz instigated the price war to reclaim much of the market share lost directly to HUK-Coburg.

"OVER BANKED" IN GERMANY

Why do financial services companies enter into price wars? According to a study by Heil (1996), overcapacity and commoditization are the two most important causes of price wars. Rolf Breuer, a member of board at Deutsche Bank, believes that "there are too many banks with too many local branches". Many markets remain "over banked", and Germany is a case in point. The country has over five times as many banks as the UK (see Figure 2.3) – there is a bank branch per 1,600 residents (the EU-average is one per 2,500 residents). The result is that the rate of consolidation has increased and over the last few

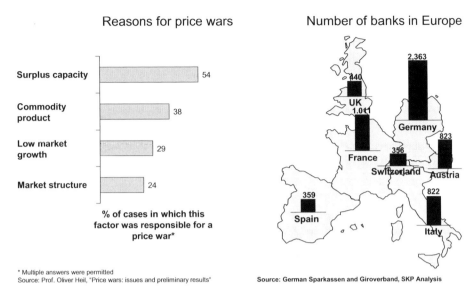

Reasons for price wars

Surplus capacity — 54

Commodity product — 38

Low market growth — 29

Market structure — 24

% of cases in which this factor was responsible for a price war*

* Multiple answers were permitted
Source: Prof. Oliver Heil, "Price wars: issues and preliminary results"

Number of banks in Europe

UK 1.011
440
Germany 2,363
France 356
Switzerland 823
Austria 822
Spain 359
Italy

Source: German Sparkassen and Giroverband, SKP Analysis

Figure 2.3   Causes of price wars

years, thousands of bank branches have been closed throughout Germany. The trend is increasing, and forecasts suggest that almost half of all German bank branches will either be closed or will merge. The last few years have seen the consolidation of Germany's credit unions rise to new heights with the total number of institutions falling and more than 57 mergers taking place. In 1990, around 3,400 credit unions were in existence, but by the end of 2007, this number fell to only 200, and is expected to continue to decline even further.

STAGNATING BANK MARKET IN THE UNITED STATES

Stagnating markets can also ignite price wars because managers often underestimate the effects of prices and instead treat prices (e.g. credit interest) as marketing weapons. The result all too often is that banks find themselves in a crisis of their own doing and typically see cost reduction measures as the only way out. Over the last five years alone, US banks have laid off more than 100,000 employees in order to keep costs down and meet their profit forecasts. Most cost saving measures have been exhausted, and few significant cost saving opportunities remain.

How can this type of crisis be avoided and how can profits be increased without such drastic cost reductions? Managers in financial services must pay more attention to prices. Today, there is far greater unexploited potential for increasing profits through pricing than through cost cutting. "Quick wins" can be made through easily implementable pricing measures. Price improvements impact margins and profit immediately and normally do not require a costly up front investment. Professional price management presents three advantages to cost cutting: time savings, avoided reorganization/outsourcing expenditure and higher profits.

Losses from price wars can reach billions in any industry, and businesses affected by price wars can take years to recover. There are several possible measures that can be taken to avoid price wars and the resulting price drops.

PREDICTING COMPETITOR REACTION

Banks and insurance companies should try and anticipate their competitors' reactions before making price changes. Certain analysis techniques can help quantify the effect of price increase scenarios and assess their consequences. It is also worth considering certain aspects of game theory in these situations. These analysis techniques help simulate competitors' behaviour in different price change scenarios and show their likely effect on market share. For example, a manager of a financial services institution was considering two strategies – attack or defend – and wanted to analyze the following questions:

Attack scenario (i.e. offering a high yield checking account):

- What strategic goals should management pursue with the new attack-oriented product offering (e.g. number of new customers, positioning, customer satisfaction, sales volume)?

- What should the new price and product offering for private customers consist of?

- In order to aggressively acquire new customers, exactly how high should the checking account deposit interest be?

- How many new customers can we expect from the new checking account offering?

- What is the price-response function for this product? How high is the price elasticity? Are there any regional differences?

- What are the customer price thresholds (from an expert judgment and customer perspective)?

- How will competitors react to the new checking account? What effects will these reactions have on our key performance indicators, such as number of customers, volumes or profit?

- What implications do these effects have on the future development of the market?

Defense scenario (i.e. offering a checking account with standard interest rates):

- What strategic goals should the bank pursue with the new defense-oriented product offering (e.g. retaining existing customers, price image, customer satisfaction, profit)?

- Which additional services (e.g. credit cards) should be included in the new offering?

- In order to retain existing customers, at what level does the deposit interest rate need to be set?

- What level of churn can be expected at different price levels?

- How will customers react to the offering and what impact will this have on key performance indicators such as number of customers or profit?

- How will competitors react to the new checking account, and what effects will this have on our sales volume and profit?

- What implications do these effects have on the future development of the market?

- What kind of signaling strategy should be developed so as to avoid a value destructive price war?

SIGNALING

Signaling is part of a financial institutions' communication strategy where indications of planned price changes are communicated to both competitors and customers. Typical examples include announcing that the goals of a price change are to strengthen, rather than aggressively build, the company's position in its core market (for price increases), or stating that savings made from cost reductions will be passed onto customers in the form of better terms (for prices decreases). Signaling can take place through various channels, including conventional media outlets, industry conferences and forums, and even web-based announcements. This process of open communication allows institutions to signal their plans and goals to the market. Signaling is a sensitive area with many regulatory and legal implications, and it is imperative to ensure that all communication is conducted under the rules and regulations governing the company.

DIFFERENTIATED PRICE STRUCTURES

Price undercutting strategies are more likely when price structures of competing companies are easily comparable. Therefore, providers should focus on creating differentiated price structures. These types of intelligent price concepts such as non-linear pricing are discussed in more detail in Chapter 5.

PRODUCT BUNDLING

Bundling various products together (e.g. checking accounts and savings accounts in one package) enables differentiation and helps avoid price wars. Companies in other industries, such as Microsoft and McDonald's, have successfully used this type of package solutions which are discussed in more detail in Chapter 5.

PROFESSIONAL MANAGEMENT OF DISCOUNTS

Clear rules and processes should govern the granting of discounts. As a first step, financial services institutions should take efforts to understand how and when discounts are currently given. Then, rules governing when and how they are granted in the future should be developed. Management should also develop special tools to enable sales personnel to calculate the effects of discounts on volume, revenue and profit. In this way, sales teams become fully aware of the need for better price enforcement (see Chapter 7).

INCENTIVISING SALESPEOPLE

Establishing the appropriate sales incentive systems is a critical step to increasing margins. Often, a salespersons' commission is based on volume, and does not account for margins. In competitive markets, salespeople will frequently achieve their sales goals by offering hefty discounts. The result is high volumes, but low margins. This trend can be easily reversed by simply introducing a profit-based incentive system.

Price as the profit driver

Profit is determined by four factors: volume, price, fixed costs and variables costs. Figure 2.4 shows the relationship between these four variables.

Whereas profit is derived from revenue less costs, revenue is the product of sales volume and price. Decision makers devote a large portion of their time to cost reduction measures (e.g. personnel or processing costs), but this leads to a one-sided focus on costs with too little attention paid to pricing.

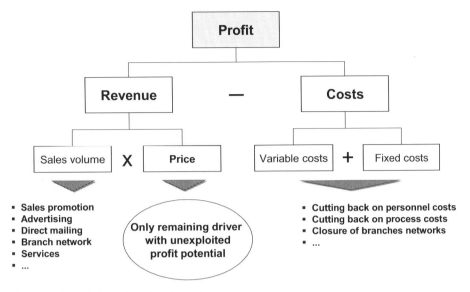

Figure 2.4   Determinants of profit

Price is the one unexploited driver of profits. On reflection, this is surprising since, as Figure 2.5 highlights, price has by far the greatest impact on profit.

Let us look at a simplified example to demonstrate pricing's leverage on profit. A US bank offers its customers a checking account with an annual fee of $100. Sales volume is one million accounts with variable costs of $80 per account while fixed costs are $10 million. The bank will earn a profit of $10 million at this price (= ($100 – $80) × $1m$ - $10m$).

The bank now decides to analyze the effect on profit of a 10 percent improvement in each of the four profit drivers (price, sales volume, variable and fixed costs). The outcome of is shown in Figure 2.5. Assuming all the other variables remain constant, a 10 percent price increase (from $100 to $110) leads to a profit increase of 100 percent, from $10 to $20 million (= ($110 – $80) × $1m$ - $10m$). The other profit drivers do not have anywhere near the same effect. A 10 percent improvement of variable costs, sales, and fixed costs result in a profit increase of 80 percent, 20 percent and 10 percent, respectively. This simplified example clearly demonstrates the rewards associated with the time and energy required to craft (intelligent) price increases, as opposed to, for example, trying to cut costs or to increase sales volume. Managers and key decision-makers should acknowledge that price (in this case the checking account fee) is the most effective profit driver, and should devote resources to optimizing it accordingly. This applies to an even greater extent the lower the margin of the specific financial services product is.

An improvement of 10 percent ... increases profit by ...

	Profit driver		Profit ($m)		
	Old	New	Old	New	
Price (account fee p.a.)	100	110	10	20	100%
Variable costs p.a.	80	72	10	18	80%
Sales volume (no. of checking accounts)	1m	1.1m	10	12	20%
Fixed costs	10m	9m	10	11	10%

> An increase in the account fee of 10 percent (from $100 to $110 p.a.) increases profit by 100 percent to $20 million.

Figure 2.5   Price, costs and sales volume as profit drivers

The following analyses further demonstrate the power of pricing:

Analysis 1: if a bank can achieve an average improvement of only 10 basis points on its deposit or credit interest rates, the impact on profit is as follows:

- On volume of $1 billion → $1 million additional annual profit,

- On volume of $10 billion → $10 million additional annual profit,

- On volume of $100 billion → $100 million additional annual profit.

Analysis 2: if a bank can achieve only $10 more per customer per year on average, it will have the following profit impact:

- 100,000 customers → $1 million additional annual profit,

- 500,000 customers → $5 million additional annual profit,

- 1,000,000 customers → $10 million additional annual profit.

Simple price-response calculation

Let us look at another example to understand the effect of changes in price on profit (see also Figure 2.6). A financial services institution offers its customer an average credit rate of 5 percent. With a credit volume of £1 billion and variable costs of 4 percent (including refinancing and risk costs), the implied margin is 1 percent (corresponding to 100 basis points). As they are not dependent on volume, fixed costs are not taken into account in this example. The institution's goal is to generate a profit of £10 million (= 0.01 × £1bn).

On the request of sales, management wanted to investigate whether the average credit interest rate of 5 percent was too high and assess the possibility of a 10 percent price reduction (i.e. a 50 basis point price reduction). How much would credit volumes have to increase for profit to remain constant? The answer: 100 percent! When reducing the price by 10 percent, the profit margin reduces by 50 percent (from 100 to 50 basis points), so in order to maintain the same profit level, the institution must double credit volumes from £1 billion to £2 billion. In other words, in order to benefit from the proposed reduction in credit interest, the price elasticity would have to be at least -10.0, which is highly unrealistic. Price elasticity is defined as the percentage change in volume divided by the percentage change in price. If, for example, a 10 percent price reduction increases volume by 10 percent, then price elasticity is -1.0 (the percentage increase in sales is exactly as large as the percentage reduction in price). The price elasticity is negative because price and sales change inversely.

In our example, the reduction in credit interest of 50 basis points does not lead to the desired credit volume increase. Analysis actually suggests that credit volume would increase by only around 20 percent to £1.2 billion, generating a profit loss of £6 million (as opposed to the desired £10 million gain). The price elasticity in this case is -2.0 (= 20 percent increase in revenue/10 percent reduction

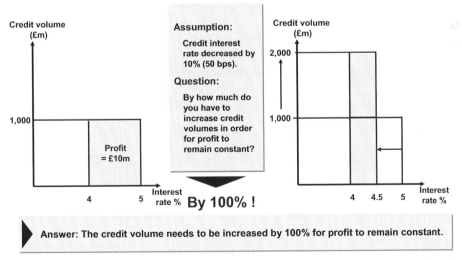

Figure 2.6   Scenario of a 10 percent decrease in credit interest (50 bps) and required increase (in credit volume) for profit to remain constant

in price). It is easy to see that, in this example, a price reduction would not be beneficial.

Figure 2.7 is a table that can support price decisions based on profit impact calculations. The cost-income ratio is shown on the horizontal axis and the intended price change is on the vertical axis. The percentages in the table indicate the percentage increase in volume that must be achieved (in the case of price decrease) or the percentage decrease in volume that can be tolerated (in the case of a price increase) to keep profit constant. Managers should only undertake a price change, if the anticipated change in sales volume is larger (price decreases) or smaller (price increases) than the corresponding percentages shown in the table. For example, with a cost-income ratio of 0.75, a 10 percent drop in price is only worthwhile if it is expected that sales will increase by more than 67 percent. In the same way, a 10 percent increase in price will only reduce profits if the volume drops by more than 29 percent. These examples show once again how price changes immediately affect profit. Since pricing measures normally do not require costly up front investment, it is all the more surprising that many managers still treat price as an alien concept and mishandle its application – price is clearly the number one profit driver.

Another example is worth considering. A financial institution has sales of £1 billion and profit of £50 million. Internal analysis showed that the prices could be increased on average by 5 percent without sales falling, resulting in a profit increase of 100 percent (from £50 to £100 million). As price increases rarely result in no losses in sales, it is essential to analyze the price-response function to validate that this profit effect occurs. This function shows the relationship between the sales volume of a product and its price. The price-response function is of key importance in optimizing prices. Figure 2.8 is an example of a price-response function of a credit card. In the example, the function has a negative slope, in other words, the higher (lower) the price is set, the lower (higher) the resulting sales volume will be.

Being familiar with the price-response function (as in Figure 2.8) is a necessity when determining optimal prices. The price-response function shown in Figure 2.8 states that: $q = 1,000,000 - 20,000 \times p$ where q is sales volume and p is price. The variable unit costs are 10 per year, and fixed costs are assumed to be negligible. At a price of 10 (covering variable costs), 800,000 credit cards must be issued to break even. However, the profit will be zero. If the price is set at 50 (the maximum price) both sales and profit will be zero. The optimal price is therefore the maximum price that customers are willing to pay. In this case the profit-optimal price will lie somewhere between 10 and 50.

Cost-Income Ratio*

Price decrease in %	0.95	0.90	0.85	0.80	0.75	0.70	0.65	0.60	0.55	0.50	0.45	0.40	0.35
	Sales volume increase in % needed to keep profit constant												
2.0	67	25	15	11	8.7	7.1	6.1	5.3	4.7	4.2	3.8	3.4	3.2
3.0	150	43	25	18	14	11	9.4	8.1	7.1	6.4	5.8	5.3	4.8
4.0	400	67	36	25	19	15	13	11	9.8	8.7	7.8	7.1	6.6
5.0		100	50	33	25	20	17	14	13	11	10	9.1	8.3
7.5		300	100	60	43	33	27	23	20	18	16	14	13
10.0			200	100	67	50	40	33	29	25	22	20	18
15.0				300	150	100	75	60	50	43	38	33	30
30.0							600	300	200	150	120	100	86
40.0									800	400	267	200	160

Cost-Income Ratio**

Price increase in %	0.95	0.90	0.85	0.80	0.75	0.70	0.65	0.60	0.55	0.50	0.45	0.40	0.35
	Sales volume decrease in % needed to keep profit constant												
2.0	29	17	12	9.1	7.4	6.3	5.4	4.8	4.3	3.8	3.5	3.2	3
3.0	38	23	17	13	11	9.1	7.9	7	6.3	5.7	5.2	4.8	4.4
4.0	44	29	21	17	14	12	10	9.1	8.2	7.4	6.8	6.3	5.8
5.0	50	33	25	20	17	14	13	11	10	9.1	8.3	7.7	7.1
7.5	60	43	33	27	23	20	18	16	14	13	12	11	10
10.0	67	50	40	33	29	25	22	20	18	17	15	14	13
15.0	75	60	50	43	38	33	30	27	25	23	21	20	19
30.0	86	75	67	60	55	50	46	43	40	38	35	33	32
40.0	89	80	73	67	62	57	53	50	47	44	42	40	38

* Example: With a cost-income ratio of 0.75 and a price decrease of 10 percent, the sales volume needs to be increased by 67 percent to keep profit constant

** Example: With a cost-income ratio of 0.75 and a price increase of 10 percent, the sales volume can be decreased by 29 percent to keep profit constant

Figure 2.7   Decision table for price changes

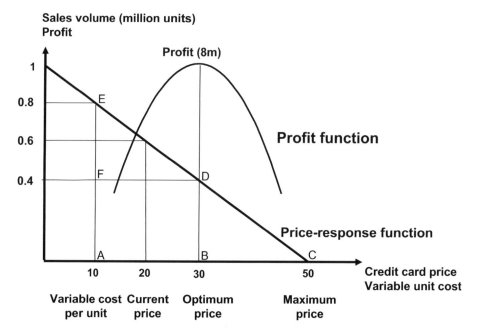

Figure 2.8   Price-response function and profit function based on a credit card example

But what is the optimal price? In a relatively simple method, look at the diagram in Figure 2.8 and find the largest rectangle that will fit into the triangle ACE. In this case, the largest possible rectangle (ABDF) is formed when the price is 30 per year. With a linear price-response function and constant variable costs (as in Figure 2.8) the optimal price (P_{opt}) can always be calculated as follows: $P_{opt} = \frac{1}{2} \times$ (Maximum price + variable costs). Thus, in our example, this would be: $P_{opt} = \frac{1}{2} \times (50 + 10) = 30$. Hence, the price of 30 per year maximizes the profit rectangle for the credit card. At this price, 400,000 credit cards are issued, and profit reaches £8 million (= (£30 - £10) × 400,000). The profit function in Figure 2.8 shows:

- There is always an optimal price (in this example, £30).

- The more the provider (of the credit card) strays from the optimal price, the steeper the profit function becomes. Changing prices further in the wrong direction would be disastrous (in terms of profit).

- Knowledge gained from a price-response function is always required to optimize prices.

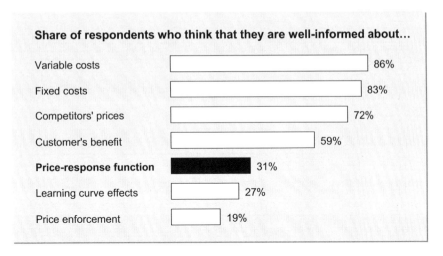

Source: Simon • Kucher & Partners study

Figure 2.9   Managers knowledge of price drivers

Do managers know the price-response functions of their products? Interviews with managers of financial services institutions suggest that price is all too often set on a cost-plus basis. The following are typical statements from financial managers: "We determine our costs and then add a margin on top"; "We don't know our price elasticity and price-response functions"; or "Price is calculated on the basis of our cost calculation". Apart from costs, decision makers often times use competitors prices to set their own prices. In most cases, pricing is determined by a mix of cost, competitors' prices and simple "rules of thumb". A study by Simon-Kucher and Partners highlighted the key difficulty in setting prices. Only 31 percent of the study participants had the necessary price-response function data (see Figure 2.9 above). In other words, they did not know the single most important function needed for optimizing prices – quite an alarming result.

Strategic Aspects of Pricing

Pricing process: from strategy to implementation

In Chapter 2, we demonstrated why price is the most important profit driver. However, simple price escalations, such as unambiguous price increases or simply instructing sales to enforce higher prices, are not normally successful.

Financial services institutions need innovative pricing strategies and comprehensive pricing processes that combine customer needs with their actual usage. Our experience suggests that many financial institutions have no set of rules, structures or measures designed to systematically set and implement prices. We recommend establishing a five stage plan that starts with defining strategic tasks and goes all the way through monitoring and controlling pricing measures (see also Figure 3.1).

Pricing processes are of crucial importance to businesses like banks and insurance companies that offer many products, and are especially critical where prices for individual transactions are determined through negotiations. Price lists in each area of banks and insurance companies often contain more than 300 individual elements. Certain areas like commercial insurance and

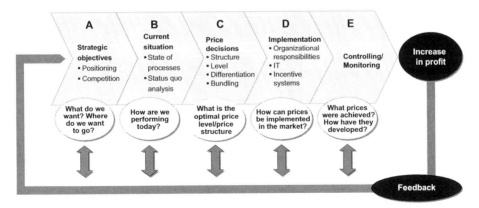

Figure 3.1   The ideal pricing process

private and corporate banking contain even more price parameters because their prices are negotiated on an individual customer basis. In all these areas, pricing managers cannot spend their time and scarce resources on individual price decisions. Instead, detailed pricing processes are needed to successfully set and implement prices. Based on our experience gained from a hundreds of pricing process projects in various areas of the financial services industry, we estimate that an improvement between 2–5 percent in cost-income ratio can typically be achieved just by professionalizing pricing processes. This can be illustrated by several real-life examples from the financial services sector (see Figure 3.2).

- A bank increased the profits of its securities business, by differentiating prices based on customer segmentation. Research has shown that while one particular group of customers react strongly to a change in prices, another segment may show no reaction at all to the same change. By coordinating prices, segmentation statistics, differentiated products and a proper communication policy, the bank achieved a clear improvement in its marketing and pricing efficiency. Bundling products into packages played a key role in differentiating the offering by segment and particularly in increasing cross-selling. The result: annual sales increased by around

Business Unit	Revenue	Starting points for profit improvement	CIR increase (percentage points)
Commercial papers	€100m	- Systematic quantification of "value-to-customer" - Application of intelligent forms of price segmentation	3.0
Retail payment transactions	€75m	- Reorganization of the pricing process - Price enforcement tool for service agents	2.8
Retail banking	€50m	- Product and price portfolio cleaning - Innovative and segment-specific value added packages	4.0
Credit cards	> €50m	- Measuring the segment-specific price elasticity - Innovative price and product structure	2.5
Private banking	> €500m	- Pricing-database development - Discount optimization (rules/processes for granting)	5.0
Private banking services	> €20m	- Development of "value added services" - Implementation of "value added strategy" (modular solutions)	3.4
Wealth management	> €250m	- Extensive pricing audit for all core products/segments - Price implementation tools	6.0
Funds	> €500m	- Audit of fund portfolio - Price optimization of over 100 funds	3.0
Corporate banking	> €250m	- Value driver development - Pricing process and value enforcement	4.0
Corporate insurance	> €450m	- Pricing process review - Innovative solution package	3.4
Life insurance	> €300m	- Value pricing - New sales process	2.6

Figure 3.2   Pricing process: selected examples

€3 million, and the cost-income ratio saw consistent improvement of 3 percentage points annually.

- Another bank succeeded in increasing the profit of its private banking business by €15 million annually by analyzing competitive pricing, customer price elasticity, segmentation options, and value drivers. A detailed examination of various products showed that the institution had no systematic process for setting prices. Each area within the bank approached price setting differently – guidelines governing pricing policy did not exist, and the price elasticities of the products were not known. Prices were normally set based on costs and competitors' prices. This project served as a pilot for how pricing would be managed in the future throughout the organization. On top of delivering optimized prices and products, it also provided valuable hints on how to proceed with pricing issues in the future.

- The private banking unit of a global bank was able to increase its profit through pragmatic analysis of price sensitivities. The bank was able to quickly and directly implement a series of profit enhancing measures using a new price structure. Within months, the increase in profit reached over $10 million.

- The corporate and private banking advisors of another global bank were too generous in granting discounts. Price discipline was at the backburner of most customer negotiations. In order to solve this problem, a clear set of rules for granting discounts, a series of arguments to be used in customer negotiations, and a new incentive system were developed. The increase in profit stemming from these process improvements reached over $20 million annually.

Strategic goals and pricing guidelines

Setting clear goals and principles for pricing and product policies forms the basis for professional pricing and is the key to establishing an efficient pricing process (as shown in Figure 3.1). This requirement may sound trivial, but the reality is that many financial institutions have complex and often unclear goals regarding price setting and lack clear guidelines for developing new packages and prices. The first stage in the process, therefore, is prioritizing strategic pricing goals.

A common conflict exists between profit and sales volumes. Most managers would prefer if their products were priced higher, but hate to lose market share or suffer drops in sales volume. Many financial institutions have explicit volume targets (number of transactions, assets under management, credit volume, etc.). For this reason, profit targets are rarely pursued as the lone goal of pricing. More commonly, banks pursue a mix of profit and sales targets, and managers are forced to balance the two against each other. This trade-off is shown in Figure 3.3. Sales volume growth is shown on the horizontal axis and profit growth on the vertical axis. The point at which the two axes intersect represents the status quo. Quadrant I represents the "manager's dream" scenario where both profit and sales increase and quadrant III represents the "manager's nightmare" scenario where both profit and sales fall. Quadrants II and IV represent trade-off zones where managers balance profit and sales goals. Profit grows while sales drop in quadrant II and profit drops while sales increase in quadrant IV. We observe many financial services companies stuck within quadrants II and IV, alternately pursuing profit and volume goals, depending on their current short term priorities. In the long term, many institutions are more concerned with increasing their share of the market than they are with growing profitably. Our view, based on hundreds of pricing projects, is that only a small number of managers seriously pursue profitable growth with a high level of commitment. The following two examples underscore this mentality.

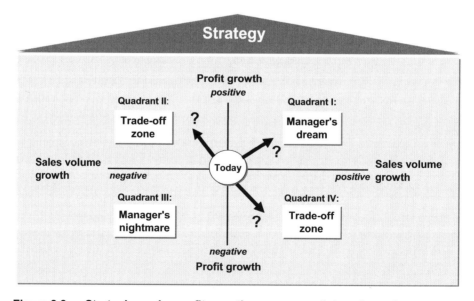

Figure 3.3   Strategic goals: profit growth versus growth in sales volume

In discussions with a leading financial institution in the UK regarding potential profit improvement measures, it became clear that there was no way around price increases. The head of marketing, vehemently opposed this notion, saying "we will lose customers!" The discussion ended there.

At another large European financial institution, the aim was an "unequivocal increase in revenues". Analysis of their systematic pricing process showed that implementing a few straightforward measures designed to increase revenue would lead to an increase of more than €40 million, but the objection of managers that this would "effect customer satisfaction" prevented many of the measures from being implemented.

These examples are indicative of the entire industry. Therefore, creating clarity of the strategic tasks and goals for pricing measures is the first step. After defining and prioritizing goals, senior management should establish a set of principles and guidelines for future pricing endeavours. These principles are the foundation of future price and product management and should be communicated as such internally.

Figure 3.4 shows a price positioning analysis of Provider A, a UK fund management company. The results indicated that the company lacked a consistent price positioning.

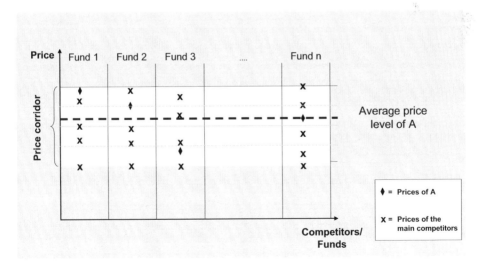

Figure 3.4   Price positioning in the market

Some products were positioned in the upper quartile (e.g. Fund 1) and others in the lowest quartile (e.g. Fund 3). When these results were openly discussed with management, the following guideline (one of ten) was agreed upon:

"We want to be positioned as a premium provider in the UK. We should set prices that reflect our exceptional service, high product quality and strong brand. In the future, our funds will be positioned in the upper price quartile."

Figure 3.5 shows an example of pricing guidelines drawn up by management of an international bank

A manager of a large European bank sums up how important it is to develop pricing guidelines very well: "It was tremendously important for us to assemble a set of pricing principles for our price and product policies. It provided us with a clearly defined framework which we could refer to in our many discussions on pricing. This helped us immensely."

Pricing guidelines should be developed as part of a multi-stage process. We recommend using corporate strategy as a basis for drawing up these guidelines. Generally, high level business strategies have no explicit connection to pricing, but they provide good insight into the strategic goals of the company. Hypotheses on pricing strategies for various customer segments (e.g. private banking, retail banking and corporate banking) can then be formulated, discussed, assessed and refined. As a result, five to ten pricing guidelines are

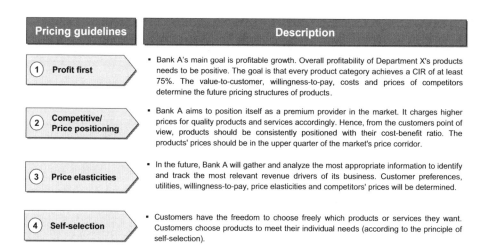

Pricing guidelines	Description
① Profit first	• Bank A's main goal is profitable growth. Overall profitability of Department X's products needs to be positive. The goal is that every product category achieves a CIR of at least 75%. The value-to-customer, willingness-to-pay, costs and prices of competitors determine the future pricing structures of products.
② Competitive/ Price positioning	• Bank A aims to position itself as a premium provider in the market. It charges higher prices for quality products and services accordingly. Hence, from the customers point of view, products should be consistently positioned with their cost-benefit ratio. The products' prices should be in the upper quarter of the market's price corridor.
③ Price elasticities	• In the future, Bank A will gather and analyze the most appropriate information to identify and track the most relevant revenue drivers of its business. Customer preferences, utilities, willingness-to-pay, price elasticities and competitors' prices will be determined.
④ Self-selection	• Customers have the freedom to choose freely which products or services they want. Customers choose products to meet their individual needs (according to the principle of self-selection).

Figure 3.5   Extract from a list of pricing guidelines

developed – the "ten commandments of pricing", so to speak. The process described above can last between 3 and 6 weeks depending on the departments involved and the "discussion culture" of the organization. It is important to involve all relevant parts of the organization early on in the process to ensure 100 percent buy-in of the guidelines. This is highlighted by one manager: "Without the involvement of our various departments, we wouldn't have been able to successfully implement these pricing guidelines and 'bring them to life' in our daily pricing decisions."

Positioning and competitive advantages

Price is becoming more important in modern competitive environments and is a key element of competitive strategies. The strategic triangle links the three entities involved in business – the institution ("us"), customers and the competition – and provides a suitable framework for analyzing competitive strategies. The position of the institution in this triangle in relation to the customer and the competition is determined by the customer utility the institution generates ("value to customer") and the prices it demands based on this value (see Figure 3.6). A successful positioning requires understanding all three points of the triangle and the relationships between them.

Classical marketing focuses on the relationship between the company and the customer. Competitive strategies focus on creating and defending competitive advantages. A strategic competitive advantage needs to fulfil the following three criteria:

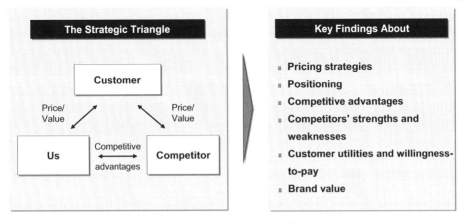

Figure 3.6   Positioning within the strategic triangle

1.   Perceived by the customer segment.

2.   Important to the customer segment.

3.   Sustainable (i.e. not easy for competitors to emulate).

Through our experience in hundreds of projects with banks and insurance companies, we have rarely been given a clear and definitive answer to a relatively simple question: "What is your competitive advantage?" Many managers are not aware that price plays a more important role than many other strategic competitive parameters. While price is often "perceived by the customer" and "'important to the customer", in order to make price a competitive advantage, superior performance has to be sustainable. This can only be achieved if the institution has a clearly lower cost base than its competitors. Without such an enduring cost advantage, competitors easily replicate aggressive price offerings.

Michael Porter introduced several "generic strategies" in his book *Competitive Strategy: Techniques for Analyzing Industries and Competitors* (1980). We apply his concepts directly to both pricing and costs in the following four case studies. In each case, a conscious decision was made regarding target markets (broad versus narrow) as well as competitive positioning (price focus versus service focus).

POSITIONING AS A GENERAL PRICE LEADER – DEUTSCHE POSTBANK

Businesses such as Wal-Mart (retail), Toyota (cars) or Deutsche Postbank (financial services) are considered general price leaders. These businesses aim for quality, reliable products at comparatively low prices in their respective markets.

Deutsche Postbank has a unique business model for a financial services company and has followed the lead of trendsetters in other industries. It is acquiring market share in Germany at a faster rate than any of its competitors by positioning itself in the marketplace with simple products and cheap prices. In the last years, it gained more than 750,000 new customers on average per year. The result: more than 15 million satisfied customers and higher pre-tax profits than its competitors. Using the Deutsche Post (the German postal system) network of branches, the bank has a presence in 9,000 locations – more than any other bank (e.g. Dresdner Bank has only 5,000 locations in Allianz agencies). Professor Wulf von Schimmelmann, the former CEO of Deutsche Postbank, explains the bank's success: "The strategic measures we have implemented in the past few years are now paying dividends. In almost all areas, Postbank has developed and secured its market position. Our particularly attractive price-value relationship, better familiarity and better brand image have enabled us to welcome many new customers." Schimmelmann went on to say, "…low prices require even lower costs. In this respect, we are almost untouchable. […] Postbank has developed an outstanding IT-platform, has developed its product portfolio based on the maxim 'simple and cheap', and has pushed sales through all available channels."

This has allowed Postbank to be on the offensive in its payment processing. For over four years, it has been offering itself as an outsourcing partner to other banks, further leveraging its IT system. It is now even processing payments for its competitors (Dresdner Bank and Deutsche Bank)!

POSITIONING AS A FOCUSED PRICE LEADER – ING DIRECT

Korean manufacturer Kia Motors, E*TRADE Financial and ING Direct are good examples of focused price setters. ING Direct's German subsidiary, ING DiBa, the oldest German direct bank, has maintained a proven business model for many years. It is a pure direct bank without any branches and meets the needs of retail customers through a strongly focused product portfolio. The strength of this strategy becomes evident when looking at ING Diba's impressive financial success. In 2003, ING DiBa acquired around one million

Table 3.1   Growth of ING Direct Germany

Key Performance Data ING Direct Germany (ING DiBa)				
	2005	**2006**	**2007**	**Δ in %***
# of customers	5.3m	6.0m	6.5m	+23
Total assets	€ 64.9bn	€ 72.8bn	€ 76.3bn	+18
Checking accounts - # of accounts - Account deposits	4.4m € 56.6bn	5.4m € 61.1bn	6.0m € 62.8bn	+36 +11
Mortgages - # of accounts - Volume	177.000 € 15.7bn	266.000 € 24.9bn	417.000 € 35.9bn	+136 +129
Consumer credits - # of accounts - Volume	283.000 € 2.2bn	309.000 € 2.5bn	310.000 € 2.5bn	+10 +14
Securities business - # of accounts - Securities volume	458.000 € 7.8bn	579.000 € 11.0bn	661.000 € 12.9bn	+44 +65

Source: 2007 Annual Report ING DiBa *two year growth, 2007 against 2005

new customers, and since then the number has grown to more than 6.5 million customers (January, 2008) with total assets around €76 billion – making it the largest direct bank in Europe. Table 3.1 shows the tremendous growth in some of the bank's core products. The best known product, its high yield checking account ("Extra-Konto") more than quadrupled from 1.3 million accounts in 2002 to more than 6 million accounts in 2008. ING DiBa also managed to grow its brokerage and fund management business. The total number of accounts reached more than 660,000 by the end of 2007 and total securities asset volume grew from €4.2 billion in 2003 to almost €13 billion in 2007. This strong growth went hand in hand with an increase in profitability. Table 3.1 shows ING DiBa's impressive and profitable growth strategy with selected financial ratios.

The impact of ING DiBa's innovative business model was expressed by a senior manager in the following way: "The growing proliferation of Internet usage as well as the decline of local bank branches over the past few years makes our direct banking model the model for the future!" Management also noted that "the most important argument for switching to a direct bank is that the vast majority of customers get better terms and conditions for high quality products and services. It is a business based on reciprocity. The customer manages his accounts online, by telephone or using a conventional letter, and in doing so, helps the bank to maintain a low cost structure. In return, the customer benefits from clearly lower prices than they would get at local branches." This demonstrates the clear and consistent benefits of a focused price leadership strategy.

ING DiBa's competitive advantages are sustainable low prices, simplicity, fairness and quality. For these reasons, ING DiBa was awarded the "Award for Excellence 2007" by Euromoney magazine. Through its clear positioning in the marketplace, ING has been able to overtake the more established German competitors including Deutsche Bank.

POSITIONING AS A GENERAL SERVICE DIFFERENTIATOR – ALLIANZ GROUP

Service differentiators focus on high quality, superior products and services in order to gain their competitive advantage. Mercedes, BMW, Deutsche Bank and Allianz are all examples of such "service differentiators". As one of the leading integrated financial services providers worldwide, the Allianz Group is serving about 80 million customers in more than 70 countries with a wide range of insurance and financial products and advisory services. Allianz focuses on four operating segments (Property/Casualty, Life/Health, Banking and Asset Management) with the vision of offering top quality products and services and gaining the highest level of customer satisfaction. Michael Diekmann, Chairman of the Board, points out, "every day represents an opportunity for us to further enhance the value of the Allianz brand. Every day is a chance to improve our service and make it more accessible. Every day we can increase customer satisfaction with our reliable and friendly customer service." With statements like this, the senior management of Allianz reinforces the company's clear focus on quality and service as well as its strong customer focus

In 2007, Allianz, with a brand value of almost $4 billion, held the 80th ranked global brand, one of the highest for any financial services institution, as reported by the Interbrand Study on Best Global Brands. Another proof of Allianz's quality strategy success is that even the difficult market circumstances of 2007 did not stop the company from recording record revenues of $102.6 billion. Year over year, operating profit improved by 5.1 percent to $10.9 billion and net income rose by 13.5 percent to $7.9 billion. Moreover, total assets under management have consistently increased over the last few years, totalling more than $760 billion in 2007.

These impressive financial results indicate that customers are willing to accept higher prices in return for Allianz's excellent service. Due to its consistently high product and service quality and its superior brand value, Allianz is able to charge a premium price in almost all of its markets – even in the highly competitive online car insurance market.

POSITIONING AS A FOCUSED SERVICE DIFFERENTIATOR – PORSCHE AND SAL. OPPENHEIM

Douglas (perfumes), Porsche (sports cars), Pictet and Sal. Oppenheim (private banks) are good examples of focused service differentiators. These niche players focus on a few specific high quality services and consulting. Porsche has for many years been the benchmark for the automotive industry. The sports car manufacturer has been focusing on innovative high end products such as the Cayenne in the luxury auto market and has been increasing its profits year after year for some time. Porsche's pre-tax profit rose from a little over €1 billion in 2003/4 to, €5.6 billion in 2006/7. In the same period, the company's annual net profit increased by a factor of 5 from €690 million to €4.2 billion!

Another great example of a business model focused on service differentiation in the financial services industry is Sal. Oppenheim Jr. & Cie. S.C.A., a private

Table 3.2   Selected financial indicators for Sal. Oppenheim

Selected financial indicators of Sal. Oppenheim	2005	2006	2007	Δ in %*
Total assets (€m)	32,029	35,347	41,090	+28
Profit after tax (€m)	250	241	255	+2
Assets under management (€bn)	123	138	152	+24
Cost-Income ratio	77.5	80.2	92.3	+19

Source: 2007 Annual Report Sal. Oppenheim *two year growth, 2007 against 2005

bank focused on asset management and investment banking, targeting the "asset and service elites".

In its 219th year of business (2007), this private bank achieved an increase in profit of 27 percent over 2004 profits of €255 million. Selected financial indicators for Sal. Oppenheim are shown in Table 3.2. Assets under management increased to €152 billion, and total assets increased by 245 percent to €41 billion in 2007.

The bank's competitive advantages are independence, partnership and the Sal. Oppenheim brand name as well as its reputation for offering holistic consulting. Customers refer to the "personal commitment of the private

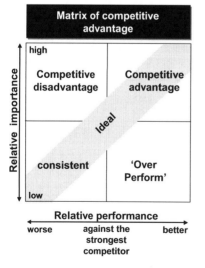

- The matrix of competitive advantage combines the relative importance of decision criteria and the relative performance of products in the market.

- The relative performance of a product is defined as the performance of a product compared to the performance of the strongest competitor.

- Strategic competitive advantages are found in the best performing products in the more important areas (upper right box).

- A consistent profile is defined by:
  - superior performance in the most important areas
  - acceptance of inferior performance in the less important areas

Figure 3.7   Matrix of competitive advantage

bankers" as the value driver for the bank, which Sal. Oppenheim expresses in its slogan: "Your success is our goal".

The competitive advantages and value drivers of a bank or insurance company are determined through the relative importance of individual customer requirements and the customers' perceptions of service quality compared to the competition (relative performance). Both of these aspects can be summarized in the "matrix of competitive advantage" (see Figure 3.7) which shows strategic competitive advantages and disadvantages, and demonstrates another important principle – that financial services institutions should strive to be strong in areas that are of above average importance to customers. This also means that financial institutions can afford to offer lesser services in less important areas. The "ideal corridor" in the matrix goes from bottom left to top right (see Figure 3.7).

The "relative importance" and "relative performance" of each criterion should be assessed in a customer questionnaire. Many methods can be used, such as direct questioning or conjoint measurement (see the following chapter for more information on methods).

The matrix of competitive advantage for a large European bank's retail business line is described below (see Figure 3.8). In order to derive the matrix, the project team, in conjunction with sales staff from various sales regions within the bank, first used a number of different information sources (benchmarking

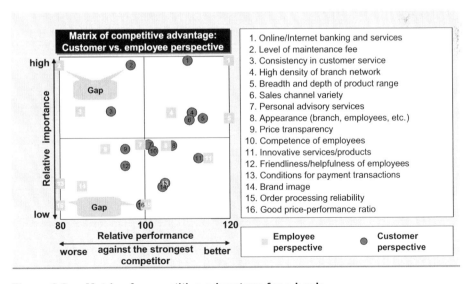

Figure 3.8   Matrix of competitive advantage for a bank

and research reports) to gather and prioritize possible differentiating factors. As a result, a list of 16 value drivers was developed and subsequently evaluated by customers and employees. Each customer gave an assessment of the importance of each factor as well as the performance of each of the relevant providers on these factors. Many of the respondents had connections with more than one bank which meant it was possible to make a direct comparison to several banks. The competitive advantages of each bank relative to the market were then represented in a matrix of competitive advantage. The factors which customers perceived as important and for which the individual bank was considered "best in class" are the company's competitive advantage.

One goal of this study was to analyze the competitive advantages from the perspective of the customer as well as the employees (see Figure 3.8). According to the employees, the bank is the market leader and has strategic competitive advantages in the three areas rated with above average importance: "online/ Internet banking and services" (point 1), "extent of branch network"(point 4) and "breadth and depth of product range" (point 5). According to customers, the bank also had another strategic competitive advantage ("sales channel variety").

From the employees' perspective, the account management fee was considered clearly too high and therefore a strategic disadvantage, but according to the customers the fee was acceptable. The considerable difference in the way that the bank's price performance is perceived by employees versus customers can be seen in the conflicting evaluation of the price-value relationship. From the customers' perspective, it was in line with the market, but from the employees', it was considered poor (see point 16 in Figure 3.8). The employees were asking for the price to be reduced when customers did not even think prices were high!

This type of information is extremely important for marketing and pricing teams. In this particular example, some prices could have been increased without endangering the perception of the bank's overall quality and service level. The value driver analysis showed customers had a higher opinion of the bank's performance than the employees themselves – an obvious illustration of a lack of employee confidence. Using the results from this matrix of competitive advantage, the bank was able to position itself better in the marketplace, to build on its strengths and to improve upon its weaknesses. The results from this analysis were discussed with sales and marketing in various workshops. Finally, the following recommended actions were developed:

Recommended action 1

In the future, the bank will regularly identify its value drivers from the perspective of both employees and customers. This enables the bank to understand the reasons for its competitive strength and enables it to communicate the value drivers internally and externally in a targeted manner.

Recommended action 2

A systematic and multi-stage process will be used to determine value drivers. In other words, all relevant functions (marketing, product management, sales, monitoring) need to be integrated into the process at an early stage. Potential value drivers are to be collected in workshops and subsequently deliberated on and prioritized. Finally, these value drivers must be assessed by customers and employees.

Recommended action 3

The bank will employ sophisticated methodologies (e.g. conjoint measurement) to determine the relative importance and the relative performance of these criteria. The matrix of competitive advantage will then identify value drivers and appropriate actions will be taken.

Recommended action 4

The results of the research on the value drivers should be used to develop specific selling arguments. These increase the motivation of sales staff which implies more consistent price setting.

Recommended action 5

The selling arguments should be tested in pilot test experiments, and success stories from these experiments should be communicated widely. This leads to greater confidence of the sales team and makes it easier to implement price changes.

Segmentation and pricing

Segmentation is defined as dividing entire markets into discrete, homogenous groups (segments) using specific criteria about the (potential) customers, such as socio-demographics, income, willingness-to-pay, product preferences or price elasticity. Theoretically, a company can treat its customers either as a whole or as individuals. Flea market vendors and car salesmen, for example, consider each customer individually and assess the willingness-to-pay of each customer that walks in front of them in order to derive an individual price. For larger sellers, however, setting an individualized price for every customer is neither practical nor economically rational. Therefore, the aim of segmentation for pricing purposes is to group like customers into different segments in such a way that differences in willingness-to-pay are minimized within each segment (and maximized across segments). Once identified, segment-specific marketing approaches and prices can be developed. The dilemma of segmentation is that only difficult to observe behavioural criteria (e.g. customer preferences or willingness-to-pay) are directly relevant for segment-specific marketing and pricing. On the other hand, socio-economic indicators (such as income or assets under management) are easier to observe, although their relevance for use in creating segments is unclear. Many financial institutions segment their customers based on such observable indicators without associating them with behavioural criteria such as preferences or price sensitivity. Bank and insurance managers should take the following steps to combine both approaches:

1.   Segments should be initially defined according to behavioural criteria (e.g. preferences).

2.   The relationships between behavioural data and general customer demographics (e.g. age, income, occupation) should be measured.

3.   The various customer segments should be described using demographic criteria which are strongly correlated with relevant behavioural criteria.

The following example shows the three step process in action: a bank is losing customers to online and direct banks who are offering very competitive prices and is faced with the challenge of repackaging its checking accounts to combat this effect. Offering each individual customer a customized package and price would obviously be both difficult to implement and unprofitable, but management was aware that the "one size fits all" approach of offering standard products to all customers neglected customer preferences. An individual customer's needs are very different from the "average customer" who, in reality, does not exist. We suggested grouping customers with relatively similar preferences in order to enable specific adaptations to services and prices. The customer segmentation was carried out using conjoint measurement to determine preference-based segments (see Chapter 4 for more on this methodology).

Through conjoint measurement it was possible to measure customers' utility and willingness-to-pay for individual banking services. Based on this information, using cluster analysis, customers with similar preferences were grouped, ensuring the preferences of each group remained distinct.

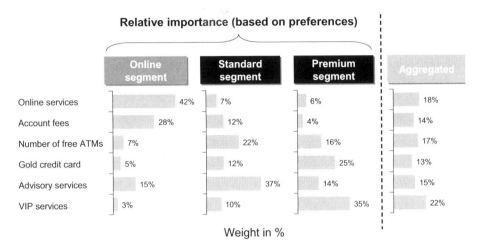

Figure 3.9   Example of segmentation

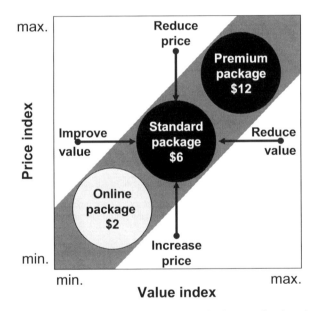

Figure 3.10   Segment-specific pricing model with three price levels

Finally, using a discriminant analysis, the segments were described using easily identifiable and observable criteria. This analysis produced one segment consisting primarily of middle-aged customers with at least a high school education and annual income over $75,000 and another segment consisting of younger customers with lower income. These easily observable customer identifiers allowed the bank to classify customers by segment and to draw conclusions about their preferences.

Figure 3.9 shows the results of a segmentation exercise for checking accounts. The bank identified three distinct segments of customers with similar utility values (benefit segmentation). Each segment was characterized by a specific customer utility profile, i.e. how important certain criteria – including price – are in their decision to purchase a checking account.

Figure 3.10 shows three pricing segments: low price, standard price, premium price segments. The low price segment is clearly detached from the other segments through its use of online service, while the premium segment has a high utility for "status products" (e.g. gold credit cards or VIP services). Using a segment-specific pricing and product design approach, the bank was able to maintain its position in the market, defend against aggressive online banks, and, at the same time, position itself as a premium provider.

Segmentation is becoming increasingly important for banks. For example, Deutsche Bank, Credit Suisse and HSBC all have initiated a movement from product to target group marketing. These European market leaders all target several groups (from young professionals to families with children to elderly customers) with customized price and product concepts.

Brand and pricing

According to the analysis of a renowned global bank, "95 percent of our business is replaceable and is thought of in the same way as commodities". When products and services come to resemble each other, banks find it necessary to differentiate themselves through their brands. This is an increasingly prevalent trend which applies to many industries, such as the telecommunications, tourism and automotive industries.

The value of a brand can be quantified in many ways. The Interbrand Study on Best Global Brands 2007 shows that, for example, Coca-Cola has a brand value of $65 billion, while Citi's is $23 billion. Other financial services companies included in the study were American Express with a brand value of $21, Merrill Lynch and HSBC with $14 billion each and JP Morgan with $11 billion. These results are informative, but seem to have little impact of the day-to-day operations of a bank. In our view, though, the brand premium is much more important. We define the premium of a brand as the price premium a financial institution can charge for its products and services based on the value associated with its brand name. A good example of this can be found in the automotive industry, where many of the leading car manufacturers use similar, almost identical, models with different brand names and price them according to the brand's value. In

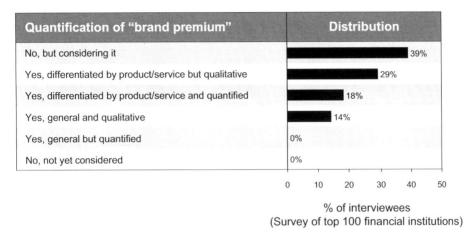

% of interviewees
(Survey of top 100 financial institutions)

Figure 3.11 Study on the quantification of "brand premium"

Europe, the VW Sharan and the Seat Alhambra vans are technically identical, but customers pay €30,000 for the VW and only €26,500 for the Seat model. The brand premium is what determines this difference. Companies with strong brands have traditionally faced the difficult task of using the value of their brands to the best effect with regard to setting prices. Financial services companies are aware that their products, when compared to competitors' with weaker brands, carry an additional price premium, but they rarely know how to quantify this premium. This concept was confirmed in a recent survey carried out among bank managers. Around 40 percent have yet to quantify the brand premium of their institution relative to competitors (see Figure 3.11).

How can banks measure their brands and price premiums reliably? The first step is to collect information on individual customers' willingness-to-pay and on drivers of brand value through a customer questionnaire. Through indirect questioning techniques, customers and non-customers of the financial institution are presented with "trade-offs" showing different product scenarios where the brand, price, and range of services differ. Depending on the selections made, the trade-offs become increasingly complex. In this way, the interviewees' individual preferences can be more clearly defined, increasing the validity of the results. Using this process, it is possible to quantify the value of the brand premium.

Figure 3.12 shows an example of a bank's quantified brand premium compared to its main competitors. According to the results of the conjoint measurement survey, Bank A's brand possesses a premium of 15 basis points over Citi, and 60 basis points over WaMu for the specific customer taking the survey. By aggregating the individual survey results, price-response functions

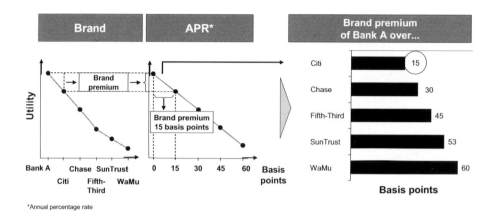

*Annual percentage rate

Figure 3.12   Determining the individual customer's brand premium

can be generated for various performance scenarios and compared to each other in a simulation model. Optimal prices can then be derived for various products and segments (e.g. high net worth private clients versus retail customers). These surveys also provide information on the drivers of the brand premium, such as the level of advisors' competence or level of customer orientation. In the final step in the process, a strategy to put these results into action must be determined – sales guidelines that help advisors identify the brand premium (using a series of filter questions) have to be created, and aids on how to communicate the brand value should be developed.

Conclusion

- Banks should completely review the way in which they set prices, as many financial institutions have no coherent pricing process – no set of rules, structures and measures designed to implement prices.

- Price management is not simply a matter of raising or reducing prices – the parameters which can be improved are far more complex. These parameters include incentives, price structures (such as multi-dimensional or non-linear prices), price bundling and differentiation.

- Setting clear and unambiguous goals and principles for pricing and product policies are the key to running efficient pricing processes and avoiding common conflicts (i.e. profit versus sales growth). Often these are not even in written form, which is crucial if they are to be developed and prioritized.

- To further improve the pricing process, it is important to increase the knowledge of pricing issues across the entire organization. Commitment from the company's senior management is vital.

- Pricing cannot be separated from cost and brand considerations, so it is common practice to pursue a mix of goals. The examples of Postbank, ING Direct, Allianz and Sal. Oppenheim prove that the general competitive strategy sets the stage for the pricing strategy (e.g. general price leadership versus service differentiation).

- To properly link pricing to the competitive strategy, knowledge of the relative importance of decision criteria is vital. These aspects can be summarized in a matrix of competitive advantages which identifies strategic competitive advantages and disadvantages. A financial institution can only survive in the long term if it has at least one competitive advantage.

- The aim of segmentation is to group customers according to certain criteria (e.g. preferences) in such a way that the customers within each group are homogenous, but as heterogeneous as possible when compared to customers in other groups. Segments can be approached using segment-specific marketing initiatives and pricing strategies. The dilemma of segmentation is that only difficult to observe behavioural criteria (e.g. customer preferences or willingness-to-pay) are directly relevant for segment-specific marketing and pricing. On the other hand, socio-economic indicators (such as income or assets under management) are easier to observe, although their relevance for use in creating segments is unclear. Many financial institutions segment their customers based on observable indicators without associating them with behavioural criteria such as preferences or price sensitivity.

- In a world where products are increasingly being compared, the quantification of brand value is vitally important in determining a supplier's price premium from the customer perspective. Currently, most financial services companies lack the necessary instruments to measure their brand premium, and developed methods are being adopted far too slowly.

Price Optimization Methods

CHAPTER 4

The revenue-risk matrix

There are many methods for managing prices intelligently. The most effective approach is usually to tailor products and pricing systems to the needs of customer segments, often referred to as price customization. The general goal of price customization is to broaden the range of products offered so that all customers can find a product suitable for them. However, pricing changes have their risks. It is fair to say that the risks of implementing incorrect pricing measures are definitely as high as the profit opportunities associated with professional pricing. This relationship is demonstrated more clearly in the revenue-risk matrix shown in Figure 4.1. This matrix enables managers to quickly and systematically assess numerous products and price components on the basis of both revenue and risk. The key message is that the greatest risk exists when price changes are implemented in highly price sensitive customer segments. Using this assessment system, managers can efficiently prioritize their price analyses. As always, the key question is, how will customers react to price changes?

As an example, an analysis of the various pricing strategies for the retail services of a global bank showed that its savings account fee had a significant impact on revenue and that customers were highly sensitive to this pricing component (high risk and high revenue, see Figure 4.1).

The reason for its high risk-high reward status was that the account fee was central to customer perception of the product, and thus was the subject of the majority of customer communication. Systematically entering price components into the matrix helped rank them according to their level of priority, clearly indicating that a reduction in the interest rate of a savings account was hardly perceived by customers, but nevertheless led to a significant increase in revenues (low risk and high revenue).

In most financial services institutions, revenue figures are easily obtained directly from finance departments. The unknown variable is the risk dimension

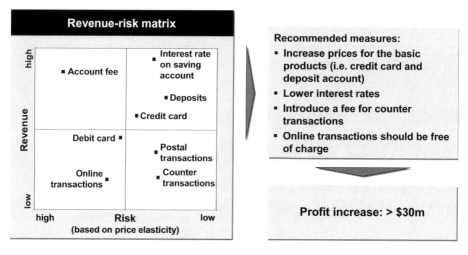

Figure 4.1   The revenue-risk matrix

of the matrix. One indicator of this risk is price elasticity. However, how can managers quantify and calculate this? What methods can financial services institutions use to reliably determine the price-response functions of their products?

Methods to determine price-response functions

In this section, various methods to measure the price elasticity of financial products, as well as to determine their corresponding price-response function will be presented. Two types of methods are demonstrated – observation-based and survey-based. The former includes price experiments (laboratory and field experiments) as well as observations of real market data. The latter approach uses surveys of industry experts and/or customers to determine price-response functions. There are two types of customer survey methods that are generally used: direct customer questioning and conjoint measurement. Figure 4.2 provides an overview of the various methods.

OBSERVATION-BASED METHODS FOR DETERMINING PRICE-RESPONSE FUNCTIONS

Price experiments

Price experiments normally involve presenting different prices to customers in real or simulated purchasing scenarios and measuring their reaction through changes in volume, revenue and profit. The data is collected through observation of real customer behaviour, not from surveys.

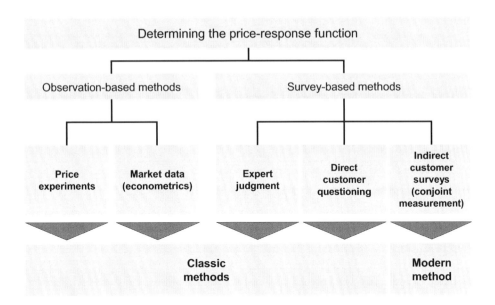

Figure 4.2   Methods for determining price-response functions

Two main types of price experiments are used in practice: laboratory experiments and field experiments. The laboratory environment is, to a large extent, artificial, and respondents are aware of the test scenario; therefore, the resulting validity is uncertain. Moreover, it is often unclear whether the subjects would behave in the same way outside laboratory conditions. From our experience, laboratory experiments are not normally suitable to conduct price experiments for financial services institutions.

These issues can be avoided by using field experiments, since they take place in a natural environment (e.g. in a bank branch office or online). Moreover, customers are often not even aware that they have been chosen as subjects of a field experiment. In one example, interest rates for selected customer checking accounts were simply raised from 0.5 percent to 1.5 percent at several branch offices of a bank, and the effects of the price change on volume were determined (e.g. number of new checking accounts or volume of deposits).

Price tests of this kind are also particularly efficient when carried out via mail. For example, one bank offered a sample of 1,000 customers a call money account at an interest rate of 2 percent. The positive customer reaction convinced management to extend the offer to all the customers. The results of field experiments offer a higher level of external validity and can be expanded with a greater degree of confidence. Also, field experiments are more valid because they provide some control over external factors that might affect the marketplace. In other words, a change in the dependent variable (e.g. deposit volume) can be more directly attributed to the manipulation of the independent variable (e.g. the interest rate) in price experiments than in lab tests. In contrast to laboratory experiments, the risk of subjects' reactive behaviour is minimized in price experiments because they are carried out in a natural environment. In summary, price experiments can be very useful for determining price-response functions. However, one key disadvantage for financial services institutions (particularly in a branch network) is the high costs and overall time required to conduct them.

Market data

Historical transaction data on volume, prices and interest rates and other marketing analytics is now increasingly available in many markets. Financial services institutions now have data warehouses dedicated to the collection and analysis of this kind of data, and the Internet has become a source of information too. Data collection has become quick and easy, enabling efficient assessment of marketing campaigns. This data can be used in econometric models to determine the price-response functions, and derive optimal price and profit levels. Regression analysis is normally used to assess econometric data, which, as historical market data, is externally very valid.

A key requirement for using market data to measure price change effects is ensuring that there is sufficient variation in past price levels. It is important to note that if the price of a product has not changed over a particular period of time, no price effect can be measured. In such situations, market data observation is not a viable method for deriving a price-response function. Figure 4.3 provides an example of a price-response function based on market data.

In practice, price experiments and market data observations offer less significant data for determining price-response functions than survey based methods.

SURVEY BASED METHODS FOR DETERMINING THE PRICE-RESPONSE FUNCTIONS

Survey based methods are either expert judgment or customer interviews. The latter can be subdivided into direct and conjoint measurement (indirect) surveys.

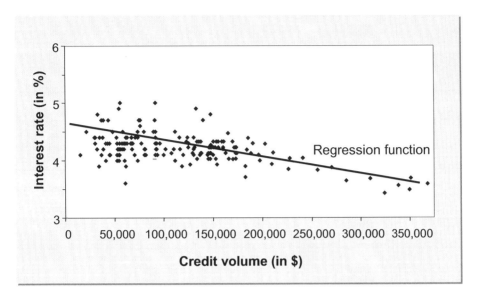

Figure 4.3   Determining the price-response function based on market data

Expert judgment

In expert judgment, individuals who are recognized as having a thorough understanding of the market, such as product managers or advisors, assess the impact of price changes on the market (customer as well as competitive changes) based on their past experience.

PriceStrat is a decision support tool, developed by Simon, Kucher & Partners, which has been successfully used to assess the impact of price variations. The model is capable of mapping customer as well as competitor reaction to price changes. Based on their market experience, internal experts are asked to forecast customer response to price changes of their own products. In order to obtain a full picture of price change effects, experts judge the impact of systematically varied price changes on sales volume. The experts are then asked to project competitor reactions and estimate the level of price change that would cause a specific competitor to react in a particular way. The PriceStrat algorithm then quantifies and aggregates the individual experts' judgments, and produces a single price-response function graph.

Fundamentally, the process summarized in Figure 4.4 attempts to answer the following questions:

- What effect do changes in the price of selected products have on their sales volume?

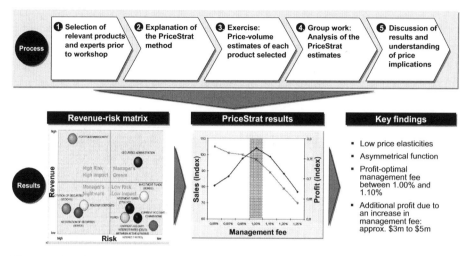

Figure 4.4   Process for an expert judgment exercise

- What changes in the competitive landscape (market share) can be expected as a result of a price change?

- How are the financial services institution's most important competitors likely to react to the price change?

- What are the price elasticities (with and without competitor reaction)?

- What effect do price changes and competitor reaction have on the revenue and profit?

The benefit of using a custom built PriceStrat tool is that it shows the quantified effects of various price changes in graphical format, thus enabling immediate further discussion and debate, ideally in a workshop setting.

The following example provides further demonstration. An international bank faced the challenge of introducing a new checking account package to the market. Opinions on the optimal level for the introductory price differed across functional areas (i.e. marketing, finance, sales). The Head of Finance suggested charging a minimum of $7 per month for the product, while sales insisted on offering the package for less than $5 per month. To determine the price-response function and resolve the conflict, 12 managers from various units (sales, marketing, etc.) were invited to participate in a workshop as market experts.

The market experts were asked to estimate the sales volume of the checking account package at different prices levels (between $5 and $12). When making their estimates, they were also required to take into account the competitive reaction. The board wanted to use one consistent price, based on these individual estimates; therefore, the functions were aggregated into a single price-response function. Based on the knowledge that the monthly variable cost per checking account unit was in the region of $4, the expected profit at each price could be estimated. The profit-optimal price turned out to be around $8 which in turn resulted in monthly profit of $3.6 million.

Based on a cost plus approach (i.e. pricing method that adds an additional amount representing profit to the cost of providing a product) the price would have been around $6 with a 50 percent margin on variable costs of $4. Had the bank set prices on this basis, as originally anticipated, it would have missed out on annual profit of around $16.5 million (($3,600,000 - $2,225,000) × 12). Hence, the optimal price generated 62 percent more profit.

The expert judgment method is particularly useful when dealing with innovative products and services or new situations (e.g. assessing the expected impact of new competitors). The method is cost-effective, quick and pragmatic. On the down side, it is based exclusively on internal information, and internal expert judgment may not always reflect actual customer behaviour. Fortunately, our experience of more than 200 implementations of this methodology worldwide, suggests that internal expert judgment in financial services institutions reflects customer and market reactions to price changes relatively well. From our experience using this tool, we have drawn the following general conclusions:

- Only choose managers to participate in expert judgments methods who are both experienced and close enough to the market to be able to accurately estimate both customer and competitor reactions to price changes.

- Ideally experts should represent all relevant internal departments (e.g. marketing, sales and finance) and regions (central headquarters versus branches).

- The optimal number of PriceStrat workshop participants is between five and ten experts.

- All results should be openly discussed, with amendments to estimates permitted, and consensus driving final decisions.

- Tools such as PriceStrat should be used to show results (price-response function, revenue function, profit function) immediately.

- The expert judgment method can be implemented in a short time frame. However, there is a risk that, if used in isolation, it may simply mirror internal errors in judgment, or political views. Hence, it should rather be considered as a way of validating the results of other methods (e.g. price experiments or customer surveys).

Figure 4.5 shows the PriceStrat results for a selection of financial services products. The first row shows the results of the case study described above. The price-response examples in the subsequent rows were also derived from expert judgment. Based on this information, profit-optimal prices and the potential profit increase were calculated.

Customer interviews

There are two approaches to customer surveys. Using the direct questioning method, customers are asked candidly about what the maximum price that they would be willing to pay for a particular product or service is. The conjoint measurement methodology, on the other hand, determines the price-response function using an indirect approach based on customer preferences.

Direct customer questioning   As part of a direct customer survey, questions like the following are asked:

- How much would you pay for this product?

Product	Relevant pricing issues	Intended/old price (index)	New price with PriceStrat (index)	Profit increase (%)
Packaged checking accounts (see text)	Cost focus	100	133	62%
Overdraft	Risk oriented	100	105	12%
Investment funds	Value driven	100	115	19%
Saving products	Competitor and cost oriented	100	92	14%
Deposits	Low price elasticity	100	112	34%
Payment transactions (B2B)	Commodity	100	95	8%
Securities advisory services	High level of innovation	100	108	15%
Life insurance	Value driven	100	118	17%
Car insurance	Product/Service differentiation	100	84/110	27%

Figure 4.5   PriceStrat results for selected banking and insurance products

- How likely is it that you would pay $75 annually for this product?

- How large must the price difference be for you to switch from product A to product B?

Answers to these and similar questions seek to determine price-response functions.

In the following example, the price-response functions for three different customer segments of a consumer credit card were examined. A new credit card was shown to customers, and its relative advantages compared to similar credit card offerings were explained in detail. Customers completed a computer-aided questionnaire designed based on a technique developed by Peter van Westendorp in the 1970s.

1. "What do you consider an expensive price to pay per year for this credit card?"

2. "What do you consider a cheap price to pay per year for this credit card?"

Figure 4.6 shows the results of this survey. Responses from both questions were graphically represented in the diagrams shown. The intersection of both functions "expensive versus cheap" is known as "indifferent" price. In other words, the price that respondents considered to be an appropriate price to pay for the credit card.

For two segments (retail and premium), this appropriate price was determined to be around $30 while the more affluent segment considered a

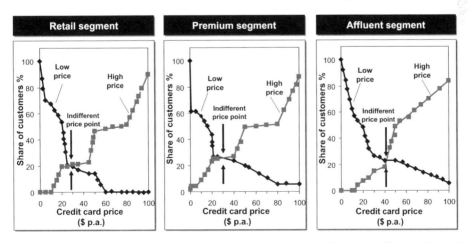

Figure 4.6   **Segment-specific price-response functions for a credit card based on a direct customer survey**

price of $40 appropriate. An expert judgment survey subsequently confirmed a price of $30 per year. The bank introduced the credit card at an annual fee of $29.90, an increase in the previous fee of $9.90. As a result, profit increased by around $3 million per year.

The direct customer questioning method is characterized by its simplicity, cost-effectiveness and speed, but it does have the following drawbacks:

- By asking directly how much a customer is willing to pay for a product, too much emphasis is placed on price, which can create unnaturally high price awareness.

- The point of a direct customer questionnaire is to analyze price in isolation. However, in reality, the customer weighs price against other factors.

- There is the risk that, in a direct survey, respondents indicate lower willingness-to-pay than they are prepared to pay in reality. Hence non-optimal (too low) prices could be recommended.

As a result of the above drawbacks, it is not recommended to rely solely on the direct customer questioning method. Rather, it should be used in conjunction with other methods.

Conjoint measurement The disadvantages of direct customer surveys described above can be avoided by utilizing the conjoint measurement method (or "indirect" survey method). In its broadest sense, conjoint measurement, often referred to as conjoint analysis, is a process of building a preference structure model using part worth utility values (the utility of different product characteristics) calculated from customer preferences (total utility value) for a selection of products and product features.

In contrast to direct questionnaires, the conjoint measurement method does not attempt to isolate customers' willingness-to-pay. Instead, it presents customers with a series of purchasing scenarios, and has them make a trade-off between price and utility. In this way, the conjoint measurement method is able to judge respondents' responses to price changes more effectively than direct questioning methods. Conjoint measurement is able to answer questions such as:

- How much is the customer willing to pay for certain banking and insurance products (e.g. travel insurance, checking account packages, life insurance)?

- How important are individual product features such as interest rates or service levels in the purchasing decision?

- How much is the customer willing to pay for certain features of a particular product?

- How much is the customer willing to pay for supplementary services (e.g. travel or accident insurance with a credit card)?

- What is the added-value of a brand compared to another?

- To what extent do customer utility values of various value propositions differ from each other? Are there as a result any pricing implications?

There are usually five steps in conjoint measurement:

1. Selecting relevant product features and attributes (e.g. speed of credit decision, interest rate, policy cover, type of advice).

2. Determining the range of values or levels for each feature (for the feature "speed of credit decision", values such as 1 week, 2 weeks, 3 weeks are used).

3. Designing and carrying out the conjoint questionnaire.

4. Deriving customer preference structures and the part worth utilities from the data.

5. Calculating a price-response function.

The results offer a starting point for price, product, and segmentation strategies. A frequent application of conjoint measurement in financial services is determining optimal price levels and value propositions. The case study below provides an example of a conjoint measurement analysis of a checking account.

Case study: conjoint analysis

A financial services institution used conjoint measurement to reposition and determine the optimal price of its checking account. Management wanted to have the following questions answered:

- How should the checking account be packaged? What features should it include?

- What is the value of the institution's brand? What premium could be charged for the brand?

- How much would customers be willing to pay for the different checking accounts?

- When making a purchasing decision, how important are the various features of the account to customers (e.g. debit card or interest rates)?

- What is the contribution of individual account features to the overall utility value of the packages, and what is the willingness-to-pay for these different features?

In order to answer these questions, a five stage project was launched:

Stage 1: A management workshop was held (including representatives from marketing, product management, and finance) to identify all potential features to be included in the new checking account. Based on competitor analysis and customer research, seven features with the highest customer value were short-listed:

1. Provider (Brand);

2. Account fee;

3. Deposit interest;

4. Credit interest;

5. Credit card;

6. Debit card;

7. Loyalty card.

Stage 2: For each of the selected features, a range of values was established. Particular attention was given to setting appropriate intervals between values. While it was important not to limit the range of values too narrowly, it was also important not to include values outside a realistic range which could skew results. With this in mind, management came up with the product features and values as set out in Table 4.1.

Stage 3: To ensure a representative sample, a pre-study quickly determined whether respondents were at all interested in purchasing a new checking account. Only respondents that were interested were subsequently invited to

Table 4.1   Conjoint measurement design for a checking account

Feature	Values
Provider (brand)	Citi, Chase, HSBC, BofA, ING Direct
Account fee	$12, $9, $6, $3, $0
Deposit interest	No interest, 1.0%, 2.0%
Credit interest	12%, 10%, 8%
Credit card	No credit card, Standard card, Gold card
Debit card	No debit card, Debit card, Debit card plus partner card
Loyalty card	Yes (loyalty program with businesses and retailers)

participate in the computer-aided conjoint interview. A conjoint method called ACA (adaptive conjoint analysis) was used for the actual conjoint interview. The advantage of a computer-aided method is that the program can automatically adjust the features shown in a question based on the respondent's answer to the previous question. In this way, all the necessary conjoint data was collected (i.e. utility values and relative importance). Figure 4.7 shows a typical ACA pair comparison of two checking accounts.

In conjoint analyses, respondents are placed in realistic every day purchasing decision scenarios. Although the monthly fees for checking account A are higher, ($6 per month), the account package offers more/better features (higher rate of deposit interest and a credit card). The respondent chooses between the $3 monthly savings from checking account B, and the higher deposit interest offered by account A, and is then asked to score his or her preference for either of the two account alternatives on a scale from 1 to 7. Based on this decision, the computer selects a new account pairing to compare, and so on. This enables the ACA program to determine the importance of the various product features in the customer's decision making process.

Which of the following checking accounts would you prefer?

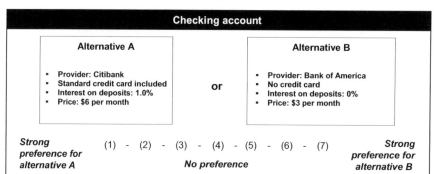

- **No direct questions about price or product attributes (high validity of results)**
- **Decomposition of bank services into important attributes, (e.g. brand, interest rate)**
- **Many levels and prices tested**
- **Analysis on an individual basis**
- **Computer-aided interviewing**

Figure 4.7   Example of an ACA pair comparison

As the respondent moves through the questionnaire, preferences for and against particular account package and services features slowly begin to emerge. By the end of the interview, the respondent is forced to make more and more difficult trade-offs, and in doing so, indirectly reveal specific product preferences and willingness-to-pay.

The product packages displayed do not necessarily have to include all features simultaneously. The number of product features can be increased during the course of the questionnaire. While the trade-off decision becomes more realistic as more features are included, it is obviously more complicated for the respondent. A conjoint questionnaire usually takes around 30 minutes to complete.

Stage 4: As a next step, using a regression analysis, utility values of the individual product features were calculated. Conjoint analysis of this type normally delivers the following insights:

1.   Utility values of individual product features.

2.   Importance of individual features in the purchasing decision making process.

3.   Customer willingness-to-pay for individual product features.

UTILITY OF INDIVIDUAL FEATURES

The utility functions of the individual features derived from the conjoint measurement analysis above are shown in Figure 4.8.

The utility functions show normalized utility values. Since scales of the utility functions are the same, each function is consequently directly comparable to the next. As an example, in the above case, the increase in customer utility value from a reduction in credit interest is exactly the same as the increase in customer utility value from moving up from a standard to a gold credit card. It follows, therefore, that the low utility value generated with a higher credit interest rate can be offset by including a gold credit card in the account package. From a willingness-to-pay perspective, this also means that a customer would be willing to pay the same for an account with 10 percent credit interest rate and a standard credit card, as for an account with 12 percent credit interest rate and a gold card.

On the highest level of aggregation, the utility values can be used to analyze the entire customer base, or on a less aggregated level, a specific customer segment, and can even be further disaggregated to an individual customer level.

From a customer segmentation perspective, segments can be formed before the conjoint analysis using descriptive data such as by age, sex, location, occupation, products and services used, or length of the customer relationship. Alternatively, customer segmentation can take place ex post based on the conjoint data. In this case, the segmentation does not use descriptive variables,

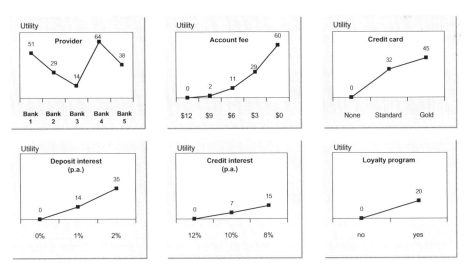

Figure 4.8   Utility functions for features of a checking account

rather it groups customers that share similar preferences for, or place a similar importance on, certain product features.

This latter method, also known as "benefit segmentation", is particularly useful in distinguishing between customers that are price sensitive, and those customers that are more quality-oriented (the "premium" segment).

In the above example, the normalization process set the least desirable level for each product feature to zero. Hence, the absolute utility function score is irrelevant. The utility value will often follow a natural path, and hence it is possible to rank the functions (from best to worst). The monthly account fee, where $3 is better than $6, and so on, is an obvious example, but other features such as debit card can be ranked similarly (branded debit card is better than a non-branded card which in turn is better than no debit card at all). Using this method, the utility values produced by the conjoint analysis can quickly be checked for "face validity". If the utility values do not follow the expected direction, then it follows that there are inconsistencies in the respondents' answers.

THE IMPORTANCE OF PRODUCT FEATURES IN CUSTOMER PURCHASING DECISIONS

If the range in utility values for a particular product feature is relatively high, it can be concluded that this feature or criteria is the most important in a customer's decision making process and that customer utility is more differentiated for this feature than for others. The (relative) importance of a feature can be determined with the following formula:

Importance of decision criteria (i) = (difference between the utility of the highest and lowest values for feature) ÷ (sum of the differences in utility for all features)

In the above case study, the relative importance of the seven product features was calculated by a mathematical program and the results are shown in Table 4.2. The account fee ended up being the most important feature with a relative importance score of 23.5 percent. By contrast, credit interest was the least important feature for the respondents. The loyalty card also scored low in terms of relative importance. This surprised management, who had recently observed competitors including this feature in their account packages. On the basis of the conjoint analysis results, management decided to exclude the loyalty card from their new account package, thereby making a considerable cost saving.

In our experience implementing conjoint analyses in various industries, the features determined to be relatively important by indirect conjoint measurement are often very different to those discovered by a direct survey. In particular, we

Table 4.2   Relative importance of the features in selecting a checking account

Feature	Relative importance
Provider (brand)	19.6%
Account fee	23.5%
Deposit interest	13.7%
Credit interest	5.9%
Credit card	17.7%
Debit card	11.8%
Loyalty card	7.8%
Total	100%

observe that the relative importance of price is consistently scored higher in direct questionnaires than in indirect questionnaires, and suggests that customers (consciously or not) often exaggerate the importance of price when asked directly.

CUSTOMER WILLINGNESS-TO-PAY

How can we derive willingness-to-pay from utility values? The willingness-to-pay per utility point is calculated as the sum of all individual maximum utility points (in the case study: a price of $12 corresponds to 269 utility points or $0.04461 per utility point). By multiplying the willingness-to-pay per utility point by the individual utility points, the utility function transforms into a willingness-to-pay function. The willingness-to-pay for a product can be estimated by adding up the willingness-to-pay functions for each individual product feature. Two examples are shown in Table 4.3.

In the example, the willingness-to-pay for the basic account and for the premium account is $3 and $6.60 per month, respectively. Based on this information, it would be reasonable to offer the basic account at $3 per month and the premium account at $6.60 per month, as long as the accounts contain the listed features in Table 4.3.

Stage 5: Based on the calculated utility and willingness-to-pay values, the price-response function can be determined for the various checking accounts. However, in order to arrive at sales volume estimates, it is necessary to devise a method of

Table 4.3   Determining the willingness-to-pay for checking account alternatives

Basic account description	Willingness-to-pay per month	Premium account description	Willingness-to-pay per month
HSBC	$1.695	HSBC	$1.695
Deposit interest – 0%	$0.00	Deposit interest – 2%	$1.564
Credit interest – 10%	$0.00	Credit interest – 12%	$2.007
Credit card – none	$1.206	Credit card – VISA	$1.338
Debit card	$0.312	Debit card with partner card	$0.00
Total willingness-to-pay	$3.033	Total willingness-to-pay	$6.601

converting a utility value into purchase probability. In this case, it was assumed that a customer would choose the checking account which offered the highest possible utility value, and price-response functions were calculated using a complex simulation model. The simulation model made it possible to examine several alternative sales volume scenarios which included the impact of competitor price reactions. An example of a complete price-response function and corresponding profit function (with fixed and variable costs factored in) for the standard checking account package, is shown in Figure 4.9. The price-response curve suggests that the optimal price for this account is around $6. Given that originally the intended price was $5, the price change would result in increased profits of 24 percent.

It is also apparent from the price-response curve shown that a price threshold exists at around the $6 mark (the price-response curve tails off to the right of this point). Ultimately, management used the model to set optimal prices and improve the overall value proposition of the checking account.

Our experience using the above methods has been very positive. However, it is worth pointing out that conjoint measurement should not be used robotically. To generate satisfactory results, we have found that a high level of experience and expertise using the method, as well as industry and market knowledge, is required. In our opinion, there is otherwise a significant risk that meaningless results are generated.

Special considerations in calculating a price-response function

Due to the complex characteristics of financial services products, determining their price-response function is particularly challenging. From the end customer's perspective, financial services products are interactive, require a high level

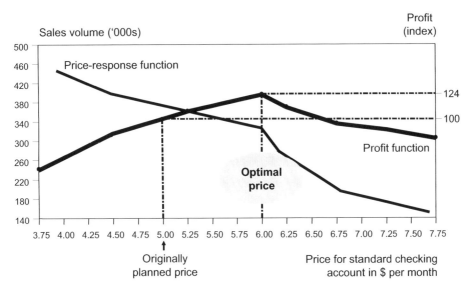

Figure 4.9   Price-response function and profit-function for the standard checking account

of mutual trust, and, in many cases, require explanation. From the provider's perspective, the challenge comes in separating out the heavy influence of the selling process on the customer's perception of overall quality of the product.

Other than cases where the end customer chooses a standardized product over the Internet, services are delivered through a process of interaction between a customer and a financial services institution. The customer perceives this interaction process as part of the service. The level of the customer's satisfaction or dissatisfaction is therefore partly determined by this process, even if it only has a limited relevance to the actual product provided.

In many ways, since financial services products are intangible, the process becomes even more important than the product itself. Unlike consumer goods and products, customers have no opportunity to inspect financial services products in advance of a purchase, and there is little opportunity to ensure that the service they will receive will match their expectations. Even post purchase, it is often impossible for the customer to objectively evaluate his or her decision: whether the chosen form of financing was actually the best or whether the investment in a certain fund was the right decision is generally only be determined by indicators, and not by the product itself. Indicators are significantly important in the purchasing decision process because customers set their expectations by them. Indicators such as historical performance data of an investment product is a typical example.

Besides past performance, other indicators may also include the reputation of a bank or insurance company; its brand, among others. There are numerous indicators that typify the interactive nature of a financial services product purchase, such as the information material provided, the branch layout or the relationship with a customer advisor.

On top of this, many financial services products need to be explained to customers, as complex investment or financing decisions often require a thorough examination of any documentation provided. Furthermore, they require an advisor to have detailed knowledge of a product and the ability to explain complex products to their customers.

To this extent, the question of what the product actually is frequently arises. Is it only the final financial product, or is the service throughout the process also relevant? Hence, when attempting to measure the price-response function for financial services products, there are three specific requirements to be taken into account:

Firstly, the product under investigation must be precisely defined. This refers both to the core service as well as to other elements mentioned above.

Secondly, the product must be fully explained to the customer so that the same level of information is available as if the customer is making an actual buying decision. However, this does not necessarily simply mean offering the maximum amount of information; the optimal set up must be decided on a case by case basis.

Thirdly, in order to measure willingness-to-pay, the actual purchasing situation must be reproduced as realistically as possible. This includes choosing the optimal surveying method as well as picking the right features and levels per feature. As discussed above, conjoint measurement is by far the best way of replicating a real purchasing decision.

Financial services institutions have a broad range of products; therefore, analyzing each product separately is neither feasible nor rational. Rather, the focus should be put on the key revenue drivers. As referred to above, the revenue-risk matrix is a suitable tool for establishing the most important levers of income.

In summary, financial services institutions face the question of what their optimal prices should be. What, at first sight, appears to be a banal question is not to be underestimated. Consider the frequent situation that the actual implemented price does not match the list price – a common occurrence when customers receive discounts on list prices. If the subsequent pricing analysis is based on these list prices, price points that have no real relevance to the market are being measured.

If, on the other hand, the survey's emphasis is on discounts, then the results may not be relevant to customers that pay attention to net price. It is possible to focus on the net price, and exclude those customers for whom the discount price is the focal point, but incorporating these differences into questionnaire designs is often technically very difficult. There is no general solution to this problem. Measuring price-response correlations of financial services products requires case by case analysis.

Conclusion

- The revenue-risk matrix allows management to make a systematic assessment of the various price and product components of a financial services institution. For example, financial services products which are highly price elastic (elasticity >1) generate a significant profit loss when the price is increased. Thus, they are categorized as risky. Essentially, high price elasticity means high risk.

- The expert judgment questionnaire is a proven, simple, pragmatic and cost-effective method for determining the price-response function for financial services products. By using tools such as PriceStrat, it is also possible to determine the profit-optimal price. It is particularly suited for innovative products and services, and when decision making comes with time pressure. However, it is exclusively based on internal sources of information and the validity of the results very much depends on the quality of the expert estimates made.

- The direct customer survey is also simple and cost-effective. The interview and analysis require neither a large investment of time nor development of sophisticated methodologies. The method does, however, have some serious drawbacks: including unrealistically high price awareness of respondents, or attempting to assess a price in isolation. Therefore, it is recommended that the method should be used in conjunction with other methods.

- Compared to the other methods, conjoint measurement is fundamentally better for determining price-response functions of financial services products. Using conjoint measurement, the financial

Assessment criteria	Price experiments	Market data	Expert judgment	Customer surveys	
				Direct questioning	Conjoint measurement
Validity	high	high	medium	rather low	high
Reliability	medium/high	low	medium/high	uncertain	high
Costs	medium/high	dependent on availability and access	very low	medium/low	medium/high
Applicability for new products	yes	no	yes	uncertain	yes
Applicability for established products	yes	yes	yes	yes	yes
Overall	appropriate	restricted applicability	very appropriate	restricted applicability	very appropriate

Figure 4.10   Overview of the methods for determining the price-response function

services institutions' customers are not directly asked about their price behaviour; the importance of price is inferred indirectly from their preferences. This method offers by far the best basis for determining optimal value based price levels for financial services products.

- Conjoint measurement can be used for innovative price models or fee structures in retail, commercial and private banking, the investment and insurance sectors, and many other financial services areas. New services and soft factors such as brand, etc. can also be analyzed. However, it must be noted that the results can be heavily influenced by the research design. Therefore, great attention should be paid to research design – the choice of preference models and the calculation of the price-response function itself.

- The price-response function: an assessment of the various methods for determining the price-response function is shown in Figure 4.10 above.

The following challenges must be overcome when measuring the price-response function:

1. The financial services product to be investigated must be precisely defined.

2. The product must be explained well to the end customer.

3. In order to measure the willingness-to-pay, the actual purchase situation must be replicated as realistically as possible.

Intelligent Price Differentiation

Fundamentals of price differentiation

Compared to employing a strict single price strategy, financial services institutions can significantly increase profits by using smart forms of price differentiation. As an example, let us assume that there are three segments in a given market that are willing to pay different annual fees for a credit card. All segments are equally large and comprise 10,000 customers. Segment A is willing to pay $40 whereas segment B is willing to pay up to $60, and segment C is willing to pay $80. The cost to the financial services institution to issue the credit card is $20. The resulting price-response function is displayed in Figure 5.1. If the institution sets the price at $80, then only segment C will buy, which means 10,000 cards will be issued; if the price is $60, then 20,000 cards will be issued since both segment C and B will buy. At a price of $40, segment A will also buy and the maximum volume of 30,000 cards will be reached. Any further decrease in price would not generate additional sales.

When determining a single, profit-optimal price, it is clear that setting the price above $80 (the "prohibitive price") will not lead to any sales, and as fixed costs remain, the company will even incur a loss. Also, it is clear that reducing the price below $40 will forego potential profit margin. Therefore, the optimum among the three options $40, $60 and $80 has to be found.

A price of $40 would generate revenues of $R = 30,000 \times 40 = 1,200,000$ with costs of $C = 30,000 \times 20 = 600,000$, and thus a profit of $P = R - C = 600,000$. If, instead, the unit price is set to $60, the profit increases to $P = 20,000 \times 60 - 20,000 \times 20 = 800,000$. If the price is further increased to $80, the profit decreases to $P = 10,000 \times 80 - 10,000 \times 20 = 600,000$. Therefore, it seems optimal for management to set the price for the credit card at $60. This is illustrated in Figure 5.1. The shaded area under the price-response function shows the achievable profit, which is the product of the profit margin ($60–$20) and the sales volume (20,000 cards).

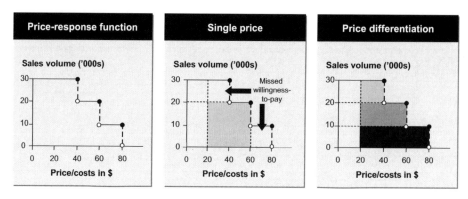

Figure 5.1   Single price strategy versus price differentiation

However, this single price strategy is actually suboptimal for the bank. Since segment A is only willing to pay $40, by setting the price at $60, the bank loses profit of $200,000 from lost sales to this segment. Segment B is prepared to pay $60 and, since this is the price charged, this segment contributes $400,000 to the overall profit. Segment C would actually be willing to pay $20 more than they are required to pay ($80 versus $60). By setting a single price, the consumer surplus, the difference between the market price and customer willingness-to-pay, is missed.

Therefore, it is more profitable to charge different prices for different segments. In order to minimize the consumer surplus, segment C should be charged $80. Segment B should pay $60, and since the price of $40 that segment A is willing to pay still generates positive profit margin, the segment should be charged $40. This adds up to a revenue of $R = 800,000 + 600,000 + 400,000 = 1,800,000$, costs of $C = 30,000 \times 20 = 600,000$, and 50 percent higher profits than under the single price system, ($1,200,000).

It is apparent that the shaded areas below the price-response function, which represent profit, are considerably larger in the right-hand graph of Figure 5.1 than in the graph in the middle. What implications for business strategy do these findings have?

First of all, it is necessary to know the customer's willingness-to-pay. In practice, this issue is underestimated, and professional analytical methods need to be used (see Chapter 4). Without advanced analytical methods, determining customer willingness-to-pay is not possible, making pricing decisions a game of luck. When charging different prices for what is in essence the same financial product, the challenge is to separately target segments of customers with differences in willingness-to-pay. Below, we further investigate the approach of "price differentiation", following the systematic approach developed by Pigou (1920) who classifies price differentiation in three different categories.

In **first degree price differentiation**, the provider is able to charge each customer a price which exactly corresponds to what he is willing to pay. This principle can be illustrated by the typical behaviour of a bazaar trader. Through individual negotiations, he always tries to close a deal at the maximum price the buyer is willing to pay. In (upmarket) private and corporate banking or commercial insurance, there are numerous products where the prices are negotiated on an individual basis (e.g. flat rate fees, all-in fees for asset management, or interest rates on time deposits). In the course of these negotiations, the sales person tries to exploit the customer's individual willingness-to-pay as fully as possible.

If pricing on an individual basis cannot be pursued and instead customers are clustered in segments that have homogeneous willingness-to-pay, second and third degree price differentiation is possible.

Price differentiation of the second degree occurs when marginally customized products are offered at different prices. The central feature of this type of differentiated price setting is self-selection by the customer. Customers are free to choose between the differently priced alternatives depending on their preferences. Numerous banks offer a slew of checking account packages (e.g. basic, standard, premium) and customers have the ability to choose the package they prefer.

Third degree price differentiation implies that the segments are completely detached, and customers' ability to choose among products or services is severely limited. For each segment a profit margin maximizing price is set. The product is only offered at this price if the customer meets certain criteria (e.g. age, asset levels, etc.). Many financial services institutions, for example, offer youth or student accounts. Wells Fargo has discounted prices for students (Wells Fargo College Checking®), Citi offers a cost-free checking account for "starters", i.e. only customers that are school pupils or work in the civil or military service get the reduced fee. All these are examples of third degree price differentiation.

Price differentiation enables financial services institutions to considerably increase profits. There are numerous examples of creative price differentiation and Figure 5.2 shows an overview of the various forms which are explored in more detail in the following sections.

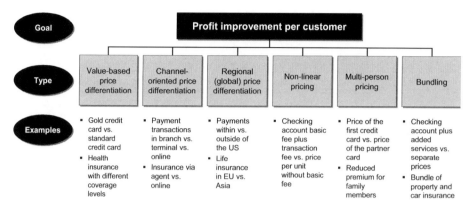

Figure 5.2   Overview of types of price differentiation

Service related price differentiation

Service related price differentiation applies if the financial servics institution offers variations of a product (e.g. a credit card) at different prices where the price differential does not correspond to the production cost differences. The bank or insurance company segments its customers with regard to how much they are willing to pay. Then, in compliance with the company's pricing policy, it aligns different product variations with individual segments so that those segments with a higher willingness-to-pay are offered those products and services which have higher prices. Key to the success of service related price differentiation is that the perceived difference in value between product variations must be large enough to justify the various prices. Some examples for service related price differentiation are provided below:

- The American Express Bank in Canada offers its customers many different credit cards which are differentiated by price and service levels. The basic American Express card is targeted towards those early on in their careers who have a gross annual income of at least C$20,000. It carries travel accident insurance of up to C$250,000 and a buyer's assurance protection plan, the equivalent to the manufacturer's original warranty. The annual fee is C$55. In addition to the standard benefits associated with the basic card, consumers with an annual income of at least C$30,000 can apply for the American Express Gold card, which offers various insurance packages, for example, flight and baggage delay insurance. The travel accident insurance coverage is C$500,000, and the annual fee for the card is C$130. The Platinum card, which is available to consumers with a minimum annual income of C$60,000, offers an even wider variety of additional benefits. With this card, customers are entitled to exclusive access to airport lounges, they are eligible for customized travel services, and receive invitations to special events. The annual fee for the Platinum card is C$399.

- Wells Fargo's Complete Advantage Package gives its users discounts on loans and mortgages and a bonus interest rate on selected linked savings accounts in addition to the benefits of a basic checking account, and carries a monthly fixed price of $12, more than double the $5 fee for a basic checking account.

With service related price differentiation, customers choose freely between product alternatives; as a result, customers segment themselves. Service related price differentiation is a form of Pigou's second degree of price differentiation.

Multi-channel pricing

The traditional way customers access their bank or insurance company has changed considerably. Instead of choosing one particular sales channel, they tend to prefer a mixture, thus having the opportunity to switch between the different channels (e.g. branches, Internet or telephone) or use them interchangeably. Channel-specific pricing has been practiced for a long time in the brokerage sector. Brokerage firms such as TD Ameritrade, Charles Schwab and Fidelity Investments differentiate their price per trade depending on whether transactions are made online, via an automated phone line or through a broker. Changes in customer behaviour force financial services institutions to offer different sales channels. Competition now exists not just between different providers, but also between individual channels of the same financial services institution. When operating in a multi-channel system, often excessive effort is put in resolving organizational and IT-related issues, while the importance of determining the optimal price structure is underestimated. Only by developing an optimized price structure across all channels, can customers be profitably channelled; therefore, before deciding on the optimal price levels, it is necessary to develop the underlying price structure.

DETERMINING THE OPTIMAL PRICE STRUCTURE

The following fundamental questions need to be addressed:

Should payment for usage be built into the product or service fee, or charged for separately?

In channel-specific pricing, the value for using a particular sales channel is normally not charged for directly; instead it is charged indirectly through the price for the service or product itself. For example, many providers differentiate their transaction fees for securities depending on how the order was placed – via Internet, automated telephone system, call center, fax, letter, or in branch. More inexpensive channels such as the Internet and automated telephone systems, are at the bottom end of the bank's pricing range, and other media (call center, fax and letter) are charged considerably higher fees (they are normally the highest for transactions done via a sales representative in the branch). Even though it is not a common practice in the financial services industry today, it is also possible to charge a direct fee for using different sales channels. This can be observed in other industries, for example, engineering companies which offer a free hotline for all customers, but charge a fee for support from a direct advisor.

Channel-specific prices or one single price across all channels?

When establishing a price structure, it is important to decide if a unified price for all sales channels should be set or if prices should be channel-specific. Practice shows that from the profit maximization perspective, setting channel-specific prices is generally more profitable than setting single prices. This is mainly due to the fact that a single price does not account for differences in price elasticity and customer willingness-to-pay for the ability to purchase through different sales channels. The resulting price potential (i.e. the consumer surplus – the difference between the actual price and what customers are willing to pay for a given product) is not fully exploited. Moreover, differences in costs (i.e. of services or transactions) for distinct channels cannot be accounted for with a single price. Against this background, if it is decided to implement channel-specific prices, some product differentiation is necessary to justify the price differences (e.g. more specific advice can be provided in the branch than over the telephone; therefore, it is rational to charge a higher price for branch purchases). A single price, in contrast, is often chosen for reasons of simplicity and transparency. With regard to channel-specific pricing, businesses generally face the decision of "differentiation versus simplicity". The solution to this dilemma is a channel-specific price and product policy which follows the principle of "self-selection". The benefit for customers is the ability to choose their optimal offer and the provider benefits from achieving fair and differentiated pricing for all segments.

Multi-component pricing: which and how many components?

In addition, when developing a price structure, it is worth considering that the price of a service can be split into various components. For online banking, this includes, for example, deposit fees, transaction fees, limit fees, and account management fees. Therefore, it is important to begin the analysis by determining the number of components that should be included in the future price structure. In this context, a decision must also be made on how to charge for information and advisory services, which are more frequently charged for separately rather than indirectly through the product price. Deutsche Bank's private bank, for example, has begun to charge a separate fee for advisory services and in return has lowered transaction fees.

DETERMINING THE PRICE LEVEL

Once the fundamental decision on the optimal price structure has been made, the next step is to examine the optimal price levels for each of the sales channel in isolation. After that, an overarching cross-channel price strategy can be developed. For isolated pricing optimization, three key aspects need to be considered: customers, costs and competition (see Figure 5.3).

Customers

In order to ensure the attractiveness of the channel strategy, it is essential to use customer preferences as the starting point for establishing prices. Product utility determines customer willingness-to-pay and ultimately, the price that will be paid. However, different customers may value the product differently; therefore, a segment-specific survey on customer assessments of the various channels and the willingness-to-pay is the foundation for channel-specific prices. As described in Chapter 4, direct questioning is one option for identifying customer utility; however, this method can draw unwanted focus to price which can distort results.

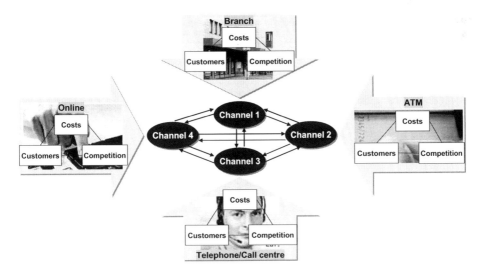

Figure 5.3   Framework for channel-specific price optimization

Another tool is conjoint measurement. This method has the advantage that customers are not asked about price directly, but are presented with different alternatives, which they evaluate on the basis of their own preferences. This generates more valid results and is, therefore, systematically used, particularly in industries where pricing is managed professionally, such as the pharmaceutical and automotive industries. These industries are benchmarks for the financial services sector. Through conjoint measurement it is possible to determine the customer utility of different sales channels and, therefore, to estimate customer willingness-to-pay as the prerequisite for setting profit-optimal prices.

The following example illustrates the results of such a conjoint measurement analysis. Conjoint measurement was used as part of an empirical study to analyze the value of alternative distribution channels for security services in private banking. The respondents were presented with several products, each with different features. Each individual feature contributed to the overall utility of the service. The product features analyzed in this specific case were the price for securities transactions, the brand (i.e. financial institution), additional information provided (i.e. reporting), and the sales channels offered. For each feature a different set of values was defined; for example, for the feature "sales channel", the values defined were Internet, branch and telephone (see Figure 5.4).

A utility value was estimated for each of the feature levels and then analyzed along with the utility values of the different price levels. Thus, customers' willingness–to-pay for the ability of using different channels could be analyzed.

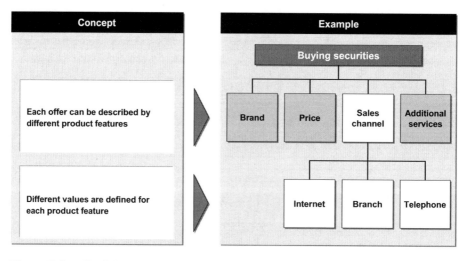

Figure 5.4   Conjoint measurement structure

Using a sophisticated price simulation tool it was possible to generate a price-response function for each product-channel combination. This enabled the bank to optimize prices for the different channels based on the value-to-customer.

Costs

Sales channels differ considerably in the structure and level of costs. It is estimated that the costs per transaction in a branch are around one hundred times higher than for online transactions. In the example above, this meant that the methodology used for determining prices based on the value-to-customer had to be extended to take cost into account. Therefore, a market simulation model that includes cost information as well as the price-response function was developed. The model generated a profit function that was used to determine profit-optimal prices.

Competitors

Situations when competitors feel compelled to duplicate price reductions in a particular channel may lead to a "downward price spiral". This happened in the online brokerage area where market providers constantly undercut each other. This type of price spiral should be avoided as it only benefits customers, and serves solely to reduce the price level and consequently the profits of the entire market. This example shows that it is clear that attention must be paid not only to the value-to-customer and costs, but also to competitors. Therefore, in the case study above, besides the utility values of a product relative to the perceived utility of a competitors' product, potential competitor reactions were also included in the model. Competitor reaction should be taken into account by adjusting the price-response function based on expert judgment.

CROSS-CHANNEL PRICING STRATEGY

Until now, the price levels for sales channels were only considered in isolation. For successful multi-channel management, it is important to have a common strategy for all channels. If the multi-channel strategy generates additional value for the customer, the channels should be managed and understood as parts of an interdependent system. Therefore, the relationships between sales channels need to be considered when setting price levels. This includes, for example, that prices must be changed if there is any unwanted migration between the channels. If such migrations cannot be prevented through product differentiation, then they must be corrected by coordinating prices. A price corridor can help here (see Figure 5.5). The individually optimized prices for each channel are entered into a system and a maximum and minimum price is set. Product or service prices that are below the minimum price must be

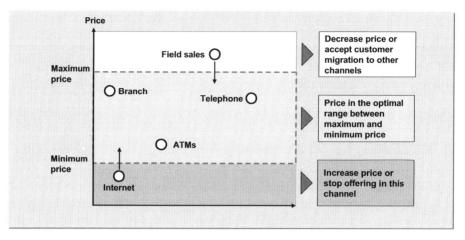

Figure 5.5   Cross channel price coordination using a price corridor

increased or else the product offering in this channel should be withdrawn. If a channel-specific price exceeds the maximum price, it must be reduced in order to prevent unwanted migration.

The critical point of setting the price corridor is determining the upper and lower boundaries, i.e. the minimum and maximum prices. This is a highly complex undertaking because, in addition to the data from the channel-specific price optimization, there are other factors that need to be considered. For example, data on market volumes in individual channels, price elasticities or possible migration tendencies must all be considered.

Global pricing

Regional price differentiation occurs when a financial services institution sets different prices for the same product by country, region or geography. This was a common situation in Europe, but as a consequence of the Euro introduction, it has become more difficult to implement a pricing policy that differentiates prices between the different countries of the European Union (EU). Consequently, for many banking products an EU-wide coordinated pricing policy has become significantly important. For example, internationally active private banking customers increasingly compare prices of asset management services across different countries, and naturally place their investments in the country with lowest fee.

Financial services institutions may seek to differentiate prices by region or country if differences in customer behaviour, purchasing power or competition suggest that a differentiated price strategy will lead to an increase in profits. Unfortunately for the banks, increasing market transparency, easier access to information, increases in customer switching propensity, and increases in their willingness to bank outside their home market, have all contributed to customers ignoring price differentiation and simply seeking out the lowest price whereever it might be. Hence, financial services institutions find themselves in a dilemma: on the one hand, they want to maintain the profit maximizing price differences between markets, and on the other hand, they want to avoid prices in all markets to slipping to the level of the lowest global price – the worst case scenario.

As a solution to this issue, a financial services institution can establish an "inter-regional price corridor". As the name suggests, this means setting a price interval with lower and upper pricing boundaries within which all country- or region-specific prices are set. The following four steps are required to determine such a price corridor:

1. *Determine the optimal country-/region-specific prices:* the first step is calculating country- or region-specific price-response functions, describing the price and volume relationship per country or region. As discussed previously, price-response functions can be estimated using historical market data, expert judgment or customer surveys (using methodologies like conjoint measurement). These optimal prices are then combined with regional-specific product costs to obtain optimal prices per country or region.

2. *Assessing risk of migration:* pricing managers should then use quantitative and qualitative methods to estimate the potential reaction to regional price differences, i.e. how likely it is that individual customers switch to other markets (with lower prices) given the differences in the country-specific prices and the extent of product differentiation.

3. *Determining the inter-regional price corridor:* if a global price problem is identified (i.e. high losses due to a relocation of assets to low price countries or regions), then prices should be increased in some regions and lowered in others. Country-specific prices should be optimized in such a way that they are all set within the pre-defined inter-regional price corridor. The following private banking case provides a good example for setting optimal inter-regional prices.

    A Swiss private bank saw its high margins and volumes in its own domestic market threatened by significantly lower prices in other global banking centers: there was up to a 33 percent difference in the management fee (equivalent to 65 basis points). Setting an optimal price corridor led to a 25 percent profit increase compared to the profit generated with a single price strategy. The graph on the left in Figure 5.6 illustrates the profit impact of the corridor, and the graph on the right describes the private banks price position before and after the inter-regional price corridor was set.

In general, the rule of thumb is: when setting the price corridor, the difference between the highest and the lowest price (i.e. the width of the corridor) should just be slightly below the cost of arbitrage. High volume markets should determine the price level, and in order to avoid price drops in larger, more profitable, markets, it may be advisable to withdraw from smaller, low-priced markets where prices are far outside the optimal price corridor.

4.   ***Introducing global price monitoring:*** to ensure that future price and market developments are recognized early on, and that measures to adapt price and product strategies are taken in a timely fashion, price monitoring systems should be introduced.

Global or regional price differentiation will only be successful if arbitrage costs are higher than the price differences between the markets. Clearly, global or regional price differentiation can be more successfully implemented if the product in question is specific to each location.

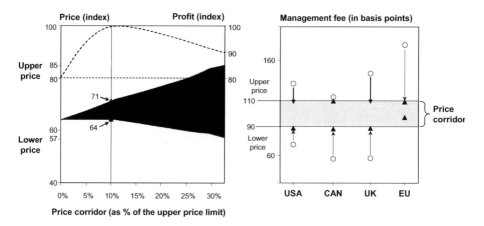

Figure 5.6   Practical example for determining the optimal price corridor

Non-linear pricing

Non-linear pricing or volume-based price differentiation occurs when a financial institution differentiates prices based on sales volume (e.g. number of trades, level of investment, or credit volume). In other words, for higher sales volumes, the price per unit is lowered (e.g. the price per trade for a customer making 100 trades per year is lower than the price per trade for a customer making 10 trades per year). A key feature of volume-based price differentiation is the non-linear relationship between the total price paid by the customer and the total sales volume. As the following examples suggest, this so-called "non-linear price formation" is common throughout the financial services industry:

- In private banking, prices are reduced as customers place more assets under management with the bank. The more assets under management, the lower the average price (in percent of AUM).

- Prices for payment services advertised on PayPal's website are a function of the seller's monthly sales through the PayPal system. For sellers who reach $100,000 in PayPal revenues, the 2.9 percent transaction value fee drops to 1.9 percent.

- Germany's Commerzbank offers an interesting play on non-linear price formation. The annual fee for credit cards is partly dependent on the total annual transaction value spent with the card. This creates an incentive to use the card more frequently, which, in turn, generates substantial transaction income for the bank.

Non-linear pricing has many forms. They include volume discounts (the discount level increases with the quantity purchased), bonus programs (customer receive benefits in return for purchases, such as with credit cards) or two-part price structures (a basic price plus variable fees).

VOLUME DISCOUNTS

Price tiers allow banks to assess discounts in line with the amount purchased, or in other words the actual average price drops as sales volume increases. Table 5.1 shows a price tier example. Management will have to decide whether, when a tier level is reached, the discount offered to the customer is an average discount for all units, or an incremental discount.

Using the example in Table 5.1, in the case of the discount that covers all units, the relevant price per trade is applied to the total volume. For example, if a customer makes 40 trades per quarter, he pays $300 (= 40 trades × 7.50 per trade).

Table 5.1   Example of volume discount of an online broker

Volume discount	
Trades per Quarter	**Price per Trade**
Up to 9	$20
10-19	$15
20-29	$10
30+	$7.50

In the case of incremental volume discounts, the tiered price is only valid to the volume at or above that tier. In the example above, for 40 trades, the customer pays a total price of $512.50 (= (9 × 20) + (10 × 15) + (10 × 10) + (11 × 7.50)). Here, the incremental discount clearly leads to higher revenues than the discount covering all units. However, it is questionable whether the assumed sales volume for both volume discount types would be the same. Each of these two non-linear pricing forms is preferable in certain situations, so it is not possible to generalize which is best. It will, in most cases, depend on customers' perception of how fair and attractive the pricing schemes are, as well as the associated effects on sales volume, revenue and profit.

BONUS PROGRAMS

The bonus program concept is a variation of volume discounts which has been increasingly used by financial institutions over the last few years. Popular programs include PremierPass by Citi, the No Hassle Miles Rewards by CapitalOne and Citizen Bank's Everyday Points System program. As an example of how these systems work, American Express customers receive membership reward points for their credit card purchases, which can be redeemed against a list of rewards, such as electronic gadgets, travel discounts or online music. The key advantage of such programs is their long term effect on customer loyalty, rather than their short-term effect.

TWO-PART PRICE STRUCTURES

This form of non-linear pricing is characterized by using two price components: a fixed (usage independent) fee and a variable (usage dependent) fee. A prominent example is the "BahnCard", Europe's largest rail loyalty card. A fixed amount is paid as a quasi "entrance fee" for a cheaper price structure. For example, a customer can buy a "BahnCard 50" and reduce the price per train ticket by 50 percent. The principle of the "BahnCard" also works in the financial services industry. An innovative price model in the credit business, for example, is charging customers a one-off fee for a guaranteed line of credit. In return, a discount on credit interest is earned. This type of arrangement facilitates planning on both sides, thus increasing demand: a study by Simon-Kucher & Partners in the SME sector showed that almost three quarters of all those questioned would shift their lines of credits to a bank offering such a pricing structure, and more than one third of the SMEs said that they would increase their credit requirements.

In order to explain the way non-linear pricing works, let us consider the following banking example: assume that three customer segments, A, B and C have a different willingness-to-pay for credit card annual fees, and thus would purchase a different number of cards (as seen in Table 5.2).

For the sake of simplicity, we assume that marginal and fixed costs are zero. Accordingly, customer segment A is willing to pay $40 for the first credit card, but only $30 for the second card, and $20 for the third card. If the provider wishes to apply a single price strategy, the optimal price would be $40. At this price, Customer A buys one credit card and Customers B and C buy two so that five credit cards in total are sold, which results in a profit of $P^{max} = 5 \times 40 = 200$.

When using volume-based price differentiation, the following steps lead to optimal prices: first the profit maximum price for the first credit card is determined. This is $P_1 = 40$ where all three customer segments buy a card since at this point they are all willing to pay at least this price or more. The resulting profit for the first card is $P_1 = 3 \times 40 = 120$. If the price of the first card was $P_1 = 45$, only Customers B and C would buy, and the profit would decrease to $P_1 = 2 \times 45 = 90$. At a price of $P_1 = 50$, only C would buy resulting in even lower profits, $P_1 = 50$. In the second step, similar to the process above, the optimal price for the second credit card is calculated. This occurs at $P_2 = 30$. All three segments

Table 5.2   Example of volume-based price differentiation

Number of credit cards	Customers' willingness-to-pay ($ p.a.)			Optimal price in $	Sales	Profit in $
	A	B	C			
1	40	50	45	40	3	120
2	30	40	40	30	3	90
3	20	10	25	20	2	40
Total					8	250
Single price strategy				40	5	200

would buy the second card, resulting in a profit of $P_2 = 3 \times 30 = 90$. At a price of $P_2 = 40$ only Customers B and C would buy and the profit would decrease to $P_2 = 2 \times 40 = 80$. The optimal price of the third unit is $P_3 = 20$. At this price customer segments B and C would buy and profit would be $P_3 = 2 \times 20 = 40$. The optimal non-linear price structure is shown in Table 5.2, resulting in total sales of eight credit cards. Customers sort themselves into the different segments by self selecting the price they prefer. By using a volume-based price differentiation, a total profit is created of $P^{max} = 120 + 90 + 40 = 250$, \$50 or 25 percent higher than the maximum profit achieved with single pricing formation.

In order to optimize non-linear price structures, financial services institutions need to know what individual customers are willing to pay for each unit of volume, that is, for the 1st, 2nd,...n-th unit. It is only possible to apply this form of price differentiation, when this information is available. In addition, as the above example shows, volume-based price differentiation makes it possible to segment markets and to better exploit customer willingness-to-pay. In this form of price differentiation, customers sort themselves into different segments (i.e. Pigou's second degree of price differentiation).

The benefits of non-linear pricing structures are numerous. In comparison to linear pricing structures, where each transaction carries the same price, it is easier to determine and exploit customer willingness-to-pay. Since this willingness normally decreases with higher usage or more volume invested, non-linear pricing structures clearly are advantageous. It is also important to note the positive effects of non-linear pricing structures on customer relationships. As each additional unit (e.g. transaction) purchased by the customer becomes cheaper, it creates an incentive for the customer to purchase more or transfer money from other banks.

Multi-person pricing

As the name suggests, multi-person pricing is a form of price differentiation based on number of people involved in the transaction.[1] For a certain number of people, the total price for a particular service is charged where the average price per person is generally lower than the price using a single price strategy. The financial services institution has three pricing strategies to choose from:

1. A single price where the price is set independent of the number of people. Here, differences in customer willingness-to-pay are not optimally exploited.

---

1   See also Simon/Wuebker 2000.

2.   Pure multi-person pricing where products are only available for a group of people, but not for individuals.

3.   Mixed multi-person pricing where the price is set both for individuals and for several people.

This latter form of pricing is increasingly being used in service businesses because consumption and delivery of the services occur simultaneously, and the danger of arbitrage can be largely averted:

- Restaurants introduce multi-person pricing for a menu where the first person pays the full price, and the second, third and fourth person pay only half the price.

- Many airlines use multi-person pricing. Southwest Airlines offers, for example, a "Friends fly free" program enabling customers to invite another person free of charge. The program is, however, only valid if booked online.

- A large international hotel offers a special rate to families, in which a family gets a 33 percent discount for a three-room apartment.

- Amusement parks, such as Disney World, and many entertainment facilities, including theatres and museums employ multi-person pricing, as families are charged lower entrance fees than the sum of fees for each individual family member.

- Health clubs offer special family rates, ranging from a 10 percent to 15 percent discount on the price of individual memberships.

Financial institutions also increasingly use this form of price differentiation as the following banking examples show:

- In Australia, American Express charges $195 per year for a Quantas American Express Premium card, and only $30 for each supplementary card on an account.

- Standard Chartered offers its Hong Kong customers a mortgage service called FamilyLink. Customers earn bonus interest when they link their family's deposit accounts to a mortgage.

- Deutsche Bank offers customers a 50 percent family discount on checking account fees, if family members (spouses, partners or children) open the same account or a higher priced package.

All of these examples have the following in common – the average price decreases the more people there are, that is, the total price paid is a non-linear function of the number of people. Why and under which conditions is multi-person pricing optimal? Let us consider the following example to answer this question: a market consists of four segments. Their corresponding willingness-to-pay for a debit-card is shown in Table 5.3.

For simplicity, both marginal and fixed costs are assumed to be zero. Furthermore, it is assumed that the willingness-to-pay of person A and B can be summed, i.e. in segment 1, person A and B are willing to pay a maximum of $95 for both debit cards, in segment 2 a total of $90 and so forth. The provider can choose from the following three pricing strategies:

- **Single pricing:** no multi-person pricing is offered. The same price is charged for each person. By using a single price, the optimal price is $P^{opt} = 35$ according to the willingness-to-pay shown in Table 5.3. At this price, persons A and B from segments 1 and 2 as well as person A from segments 3 and 4 buy the card because their respective maximum willingness-to-pay is higher or equal to the actual market price. A total profit of $P^{max} = 6{\times}35 = 210$ results.

- **Pure multi-person pricing:** multi-person pricing is offered exclusively, that is, an individual customer cannot buy the card. Based on our example above, the optimal pure multi-person price is $P^{opt} = 55$. At this price, all four segments buy the package. The optimal total profit is $P^{max} = 4{\times}55 = 220$, about 5 percent higher than the maximal profit under a single price strategy. The reason for the increase in profit from $210 to $220 is the additional willingness-to-pay being exploited by multi-person pricing. The bank or insurance company sets the multi-person price in such a way that the "excess" that a customer is willing to pay is transferred from one person to the other.

Table 5.3   **Willingness-to-pay of person A, person B and their sum (A+B)**

	Customer willingness-to-pay for a debit card (in $ per year)		
Segment	Person A	Person B	Total
1	60	35	95
2	50	40	90
3	55	15	70
4	45	10	55

- **Mixed multi-person pricing:** here, a single price as well as a multi-person price is determined. In the example above, an optimal single price of $P^{opt} = 45$ and an optimal multi-person price of, $P^{opt} = 90$ can be determined. Table 5.3 shows that for both of these prices, segments 1 and 2 buy the multi-person product, and Customer A from segments 3 and 4 buy the product. Therefore, the optimal total profit of the provider amounts to $P^{max} = 2{\times}90 + 2{\times}45 = 270$, which is higher than the profit for the single price (+29 percent) and for the pure multi-person price (+23 percent).

Mixed multi-person pricing is, in this example, the most profitable pricing strategy. It leads to a considerable improvement in market segmentation and in the amount of consumer surplus being exploited. Similar to non-linear pricing, in this form of price differentiation customers segment themselves (i.e. second degree price differentiation according to Pigou's is used). However, when multi-person offers refer to specific groups (e.g. families or employees of a company), multi-person pricing represents Pigou's third degree of price differentiation.

Price bundling

Banking and insurance customers have become ever more demanding. With increased competition from online banks, growing market transparency and greater consumer confidence, many financial services customers have turned into "cherry-pickers" who have relationships with multiple institutions, and purchase only a small portion of their financial products from each bank, based on evaluation of price-performance ratios. Today, many customers have their checking account with one provider free of charge and trade securities via an online bank, which charges them a low transaction fee. This cherry-picking mentality is a growing problem for financial services institutions because the common strategy of offering loss-generating products such as a free checking account, meant to attract customers, is only profitable if the bank can generate cross-sales of some sort. In other words, the strategy behind offering a free checking account is to lock a customer in, and increase the likelihood that he purchases additional services with higher margins from that same provider. The strategy's imperfections become clear if instead the customer purchases other financial services from different institutions ("cherry-picking").

One possibility of solving this problem is bundling products and services. We speak of price bundling when two or more products/services are sold in a package for one price. Bundling is an intelligent form of price differentiation and is increasingly used by companies in all industries, as the following examples demonstrate:

- In the computer industry, hardware and software packages are offered, for example, Dell with its hardware bundles or Microsoft with its office software packages. The potential for product bundling can clearly be observed in Microsoft's strategy. By smartly bundling individual software applications into the MS Office packages, they have extended its dominance in word processing (Word), spreadsheets (Excel), graphics (PowerPoint) and databases (Access). This strategy increased Microsoft's market share to more than 80 percent, a quasi-monopolistic position, and has set the standard for application software.

- In the fast-food industry, McDonalds has been offering "Value Menus" for several years now.

- Telecom providers such as Verizon and T-Online have increasingly been focusing on combining connectivity services with other services (GPS navigation, sports updates, etc.).

- Car manufacturers offer several packages (e.g. security, comfort or sport packages) in most models.

Following the success of other industries, banks and insurance companies are also increasingly offering packaged solutions as well:

- Probably the best-known banking price bundle is the checking account. A bundle of many different services such as an account, debit and credit payments, ATM withdrawals, overdraft facilities, standing orders, payment transfers, etc. are offered for one single monthly fee. In the past, these services may have been priced with a two-part price structure comprising a fee for the checking account and individual transaction prices.

- For cards, the most widespread form of bundling is bundling credit or debit cards with insurance services. Citi, for example, links its AAdvantage Cards with a wide range of insurance services, such as auto rental insurance, and a travel insurance. Cleverly, the insurance protection only kicks in when travel is paid for using the credit card.

- UBS bundles private banking services with free access to the so-called UBS Key Club. Membership to this club gives access to a wide range of services which are only indirectly related to banking services. For every transaction carried out through UBS, customers automatically collect bonus points which can be spent on gifts.

- Private Banks cater to high net worth individuals, offering full service solutions at one all-in price, including, wealth management services, relationship management, investment and tax advice, financial planning, and even concierge services.

These examples provide a brief look into price bundling in financial services. Below, we show how bundling can be systematized.

BUNDLING OF BANKING PRODUCTS

In the past, customers could only acquire individual products/services and had to pay for them separately. Today, many financial services institutions offer bundles of several different products or services. Normally, an entry product, like a checking account or savings account, is combined with additional service such as a credit card, trading accounts or loans. Increasingly, more innovative bundles, like investment funds together with saving products, or checking accounts with discounts on consumer loans, are offered.

BUNDLING OF BANKING AND INSURANCE PRODUCTS

As part of the bankassurance strategy, in addition to purely banking based combinations, more extended packages including insurance products have been entering the market. The combination of credit cards with insurance products is one example. CreditSuisse has gone one step further by attempting to cover all property needs in one package – a combined mortgage, life and property insurance offering.

BUNDLING OF BANKING, INSURANCE AND ADDITIONAL PRODUCTS

Bundled packages are often supplemented with additional services that are not directly related to core services. Since the basic products in the financial services sector are relatively homogenous, supplementary products and services are used to differentiate an offering from the competition. These additional products and services may include benefits very far from financial services, like travel and leisure items. A good example of a bundle which combines banking, insurance and supplementary services is the Bonviva package from CreditSuisse, which is available to customers with minimum investable assets of 25,000 CHF or a mortgage of at least 200,000 CHF. The package includes a free personal checking account, a credit card with 50 percent discount on the first year's annual fee, a free Maestro (debit) card, and a high interest savings account as well as commission free travellers cheques. The Bonviva package is supplemented with discounts on Winterthur insurance products and additional services that range from cheap rates for car leases to discounts on hotels and restaurants, emergency document registration and emergency cash services. This kind of bundling approach is often associated with bonus programs and is widely used throughout the financial services industry. In the US, Chase, Citi and Bank of America all offer packages which bundle bank products (checking accounts, credit cards) with insurance products and additional security, travel and leisure services.

The main advantages that make bundling concepts so beneficial for banks and insurance companies are:

BUNDLING ADVANTAGES FROM A PROVIDER'S PERSPECTIVE

1. *Increase in revenue and profit due to better extraction of customer willingness-to-pay:* by bundling products, unexploited willingness-to-pay is transferred from one product to other products in the bundle. This is demonstrated by the following example from the financial services sector: a retail bank decided to bundle its checking account with its deposit account, necessitating the need for an optimal price for the individual products as well as for the package as a whole.

   Needs-based cluster analysis identified four customer segments of approximately the same size. Figure 5.7 summarizes the maximum willingness-to-pay for each product and each segment. While the willingness-to-pay of deposit accounts was highest in segment 1, the willingness-to-pay for checking accounts was highest in segment 4. Setting prices for the accounts individually resulted in an optimal monthly price of $8 for the deposit account and $8.50 for the checking account. At these prices, two segments would buy one of the accounts each, generating a monthly revenue of $33 (= 2 × 8 + 2 × 8.5). The optimal price of the bundle is at $10.50 per month. At this price, all four segments would purchase and the monthly revenue would be $42. Despite the fact that the optimal bundle price ($10.50) is more than 30 percent lower than the sum of the optimal individual product prices ($16.50), more than a 30 percent increase in revenue is generated compared to the individual price approach. By utilizing price bundling, the market is divided into two segments: buyers and non-buyers of the bundle. In this example, all the customers fit into the first segment (buyers). Pure price bundling thus reduces the heterogeneity of demand.

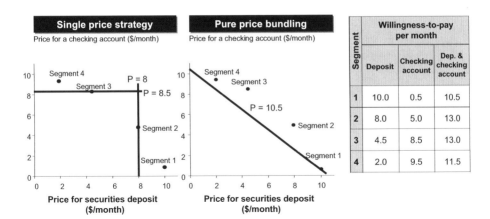

Figure 5.7   Example of price bundling

A mixed price bundling approach would lead to an optimal price for the deposit account of $p_D^{opt} = 10$ and an optimal price for the checking account of $p_G^{opt} = 9.5$. In this case, the optimal bundle price would be $p_{D+G}^{opt} = 13$. At these prices, segments 2 and 3 would purchase the bundle whereas segment 1 would only buy the deposit account and segment 4 only the checking account. Hence, the total revenue for the bank totalled $G^{max} = 2 \times 13 + 10 + 9.5 = 45.5$, exceeding revenues from the individual pricing approach by 38 percent and revenues from pure price bundling by 8 percent. In this case, the mixed price bundling approach is clearly the most profitable pricing strategy, and it enables a considerable improvement in market segmentation and a greater extraction of consumer surplus. Table 5.4 summarizes the optimal values (prices, sales volume and revenue) that were derived using single pricing, pure price bundling and mixed price bundling approaches.

Bundling is not *always* optimal from a profit perspective. The key to successful bundling is knowledge of how willingness-to-pay varies across customer segments, the size of the respective segments, and the costs associated with the bundled offering.

2.   *Increase in profit through higher sales and cross-selling:* as shown above, bundling leads to a higher level of cross-selling and thus an increase in sales: instead of two products, four units are sold in the end. This is because the optimal bundle price is lower than the sum of the individual prices ($10.50 and $13 versus $16.50). Microsoft provides a good example of successful cross-selling using a bundling strategy. As one of the most important parts of Microsoft's corporate strategy, the company has significantly

Table 5.4   Optimal prices, sales volumes and revenue for the three price strategies

Price strategy	Optimal prices (in $)			Resulting sales (volume)			Revenue (in $)
	p_D^{opt}	p_G^{opt}	p_{D+G}^{opt}	q_D^{opt}	q_G^{opt}	q_{D+G}^{opt}	(Index)
Individual pricing	8	8.50	-	2	2	-	33 (100)
Pure price bundling	-	-	10.50	-	-	4	42 (127)
Mixed price bundling	10	9.50	13	1	1	2	45.50 (138)

increased the market share of their products Word, Excel, PowerPoint and Access by bundling them into one single package – Microsoft Office. Bundling services can thus increase sales of products with low demand. This is especially relevant in the financial services sector. With the emergence of direct banks, competition and price pressure have increased significantly throughout the industry. This is particularly true for key products such as checking accounts and savings accounts. Since customers perceive price to be the key decision factor in these product areas, competing on price alone ultimately leads to price wars. Instead, bundling such products together with other products or services can actually increase customers' willingness-to-pay. This approach reduces, and potentially eliminates, 'cherry-picking'

3. *Avoiding price wars:* as suggested above, bundling can help financial services institutions reduce the comparability of their offering to competitors' offerings, thereby reducing the number of competitors by shifting competition away from individual products and towards bundles. The financial services institution thus positions itself as a "solution provider" rather than just a seller of individual products and services.

4. *Reduction in costs:* combining products and services into a single package can also reduce production complexity and costs. The provider often benefits from synergies which can be passed on to customers in the form of discounts. For example, in the 1980s car manufacturer Chrysler was able to reduce the number of different interior furnishings for its Dodge Omni and Plymouth Horizon models from over 8 million to just 42 through extensive bundling.

The cost savings in the production process made it possible to offer a discount of around 10 percent on these models. Similar synergies can be realized by financial services institutions by, for example, lowering distribution, communication and back office administration costs. As different services are sold together, rather than in several stages, synergies can be realized and savings on personnel and transaction costs be made. Empirical studies also point out that customer inclination to switch financial services providers reduces with more products purchased from the same provider. Emotional and economic barriers also make switching less likely, making customers more likely to remain with their existing provider.

BUNDLING ADVANTAGES FROM A CUSTOMER'S PERSPECTIVE

Product bundles offer customers a variety of benefits. On one hand, there is the convenience factor – customer's benefit from a "one stop shop" to fill their financial needs. This leads to ease of use, saves on transaction costs, reduces complexity and makes gaining an overall view of the individual's financial situation easier. In addition, customers can generally purchase the package for a considerably lower price than the cumulative price of the separate products or services. This leads to a greater customer satisfaction and stronger customer relationship (see also Figure 5.8).

In our experience, despite all the benefits of bundling, the process can fail if the following success factors are not adhered to:

Success factor 1: creating the package (bundle design)

The main determinant of success in bundling is the way in which different services are combined into the package. This task can be approached in two ways: from the provider's perspective and from the customer's perspective. From the provider's perspective, the objective is to supplement the "must-have products" with less attractive items to increase sales. Both the Microsoft Office package and McDonald's menus are good examples of this principle.

When creating a package from the provider's perspective, there is a risk that customer requirements are not considered and if the package contains too many less attractive features, customers may decide to purchase the "must-have product" separately – from someone else. For the bundle to be profitable it is necessary to blend both perspectives. To begin with, the target customer segments need to be clearly defined, and often multiple customer segments will need to be offered several different bundles at various price levels.

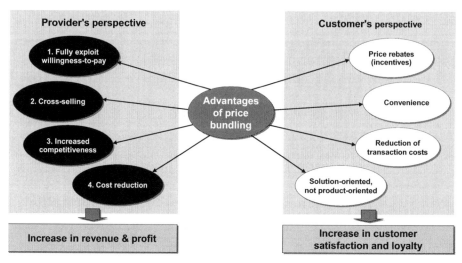

Figure 5.8   Advantages of price bundling

Customer needs are central when creating a demand-oriented bundle. Airline companies, for example, commonly try to attract customers with additional products and services to establish a closer relationship between customer and airline. Similarly, financial services providers can create bundles with different services around a specific customer need, for example financial security. This may consist of a range of services like insurance policies, investment products, tax and inheritance advice, or 24-hour emergency help and support services. It is often beneficial to address customers at an emotional level, thereby increasing customers' emotional connection to their provider and making comparisons with other financial services institutions more difficult.

Once the core banking and insurance products to be included in the bundle are selected, the question of which auxiliary services should be added can be addressed. These additional services should provide the customer with extra benefit and make it easier for the financial services institution to differentiate itself from competitors. Since the core banking and insurance products are very homogenous, and competition is often focused on the pricing aspects of these products, by including additional services, customer focus can be shifted away from price. For the package to be a success, it is important that customers find the additional services included attractive, and different than competitors' offers.

It should be pointed out that, in practice, the additional services offered by banks in their bundles are still very similar to each other. Emergency services, discounts on hotels or tickets are included in almost every package, and since they are interchangeable, these additional services normally do little to create a competitive edge. Providers should carefully select the rights services, be as innovative as possible in developing bundles, and avoid simply copying competitors' packages.

European financial services institutions offer a good benchmark for bundling. In the UK, for example, NatWest's Advantage Premium and Advantage Gold packages bundle lower credit interest rates and discounts on home insurance with other supplementary services such as low price guarantees for non-bank products.

Success factor 2: multi-stage evaluation process for the services to be bundled

Selecting the proper services to be included in the bundle requires a multi-stage process. First, all appropriate products should be short-listed – a brainstorming session with the product managers may be appropriate for this. Then, the right mix of strong "leader products" and less demanded "filler products" from the short list must be determined. Focus groups can provide the first assessment of how attractive the package is for the target segment in the market. This should always be complemented with a more detailed market research analysis. Conjoint measurement may be suitable for this analysis, since it can measure utility values for the different package components, and can help to create the optimal combination of package elements.

Success factor 3: package pricing (optimal price structure and level)

Pricing is by far the most important factor for successful bundling. It is necessary to design a suitable price structure before optimizing the price level. There are two options for price structures in bundling: (a) a single price for the package, covering all components within the bundle, or (b) a "product menu" in which the price is determined by the type and number of services selected. Which of these options is more appropriate depends on many parameters including the company's goals, customer needs and any possible legal restrictions.

Having established a price structure, the optimal price level can be determined. In order to motivate customers to buy the bundle, the price offered is usually lower than the sum of the individual prices of the products/ services included. Experience from different industries shows that the optimal bundle discount lies between 5 and 15 percent, but, in most cases, depends on the number of components purchased. The alternative is to charge a non discounted price and instead offer higher quality products and services (e.g. interest bonuses). Either way, it is important to be aware of price thresholds.

Furthermore, empirical data suggests that a mixed price bundle, where services can be purchased either as a package or separately, tends to produce better results than pure bundling where the services can only be purchased in packaged form. Clearly, the danger exists that if certain elements of the bundle are not attractive enough to customers, some will choose not to buy the package. In these situations, it is best practice to differentiate prices based on the number of products purchased. As mentioned above, conjoint measurement is a useful tool to exploit the full profit potential of bundling. Conjoint measurement makes it possible to evaluate the importance of individual elements of the package and to determine the utility value of these elements as perceived by customers. Since utility values can be converted into willingness-to-pay, measuring them should be regarded as a prerequisite for setting profit-optimal prices. Moreover, conjoint measurement helps to determine which modifications in the composition of the package would result in higher utility for customers, and what customers are willing to pay for the amended package. This insight can then be used in a market simulation model to set profit-optimal prices.

Success factor 4: accounting for regulatory and legal restrictions

A successful bundling strategy not only requires the creation and pricing of packages, but should also take any applicable regulatory and legal restrictions into account. Of particular relevance here is how discounts and incentives are offered in combination with the bundle. Regardless of the jurisdiction, the freedom with which providers can create and price bundles will, to an extent, face some restrictions. In fact, over the last decade these restrictions have tended to grow, and have led many product packages to be amended or even withdrawn from the marketplace. In most of these cases, the problem has involved packages that bundle expensive with less expensive products. From a legislative point of view, the concern is when the less expensive product cannot be bought without the expensive product. A classic case is Microsoft's Office package which, as previously mentioned, has made certain less expensive products only available though the purchase of the entire Office package. This strategy has led to the EU commission to fine Microsoft to the tune of €900 million. Our advice is to be fully aware of any regulatory and legal restrictions before a bundle is developed. In most cases, regulatory and legal concerns can be satisfied by using a mixed bundling strategy, in which there is always an option to purchase the individual products and services along with the packaged bundle.

Success factor 5: setting internal requirements

Bundles are often comprised of products or services from different profit centers or business units in the organization, and since package prices are usually set below the combined total of the individual product and service prices, any margin loss needs to be shared by the contributing profit centres. Deciding how losses are divided can often cause internal conflicts, and a suitable internal cost allocation structure should be agreed on from the beginning of the process.

Since providing customers with competent advice is often the key to selling financial services products, comprehensive personnel training in all aspects of the products and services included in the package should be provided. For example, a bundle provided by a bank may include insurance services which the bank's sales team may not be familiar with. Hence adequate training will be required so that the sales team will be competent enough to be able to clarify any issues during a sales conversation. Furthermore, a suitable incentive system is needed for the sales staff. The design of the incentive system is particularly important if a bundle consists of both banking and insurance products. In this case, the incentive system must ensure that sales people do not focus on one of the two areas exclusively, but instead must encourage them to focus on both product areas. It is vital for the success of the bundle that sales people think and act in the interests of the whole organization, rather than just their product area.

Success factor 6: management of a complex bundling process

Bundling different financial services products into attractive packages is a challenging task, and from our diverse project experience it is evident that businesses often lack the knowledge and skills to manage this complex bundling process (i.e. selection of products, determination of customer willingness-to-pay, sizing of customer segments, building simulation and optimization models and dealing with legal/regulatory issues). A key success factor is being able to manage this process and developing creative well thought out bundling concepts that meet customers' desires and are optimally priced.

Other forms of price differentiation

Besides the innovative forms of price differentiation outlined in the above section, there are several other forms of price differentiation worth noting.

PRICE DIFFERENTIATION BASED ON CUSTOMER CHARACTERISTICS

Price differentiation based on customer characteristics is when the price of a financial services product is governed by descriptive characteristics of the customer segment (such as age or profession). This form of price differentiation is very suitable for service-based businesses such as travel or financial services. The following descriptive characteristics are most commonly used:

- Age: most banks have checking account product versions targeted at children and/or students, with the aim being to acquire a customer at an early age and allow them to progress from one account to the next as they grow older.

- Education: Sovereign Bank in the U.S., among many others, offers students a free checking account bundled with a debit and credit card, all with no annual fees.

- Profession: insurance companies, for example, offer special products and prices that target certain professions.

It is relatively straight forward to segment a market by descriptive characteristics. However, this kind of segmentation can incur high costs associated with monitoring customer eligibility for a product.

TIME-BASED PRICE DIFFERENTIATION

Time-based price differentiation is when the price of a financial services product depends on the time that the transaction takes place (day, week or year). Time-based price differentiation often plays a key role in service industries, and is frequently used to segment a market by capacity utilisation. Energy providers (night versus day rates), telephone companies (peak versus off-peak prices), airlines (weekday versus weekend prices) or tour operators (main versus off-season) are obvious examples of time-based price differentiation. In most of these cases, the market segmentation is effective because time-based arbitrage is not feasible. However, even though there have been initiatives to do so, (e.g. lower prices for ATM usage on weekends), time-based price differentiation is rarely used in the financial services sector.

Management recommendations

To successfully implement price differentiation, the following recommendations should be considered:

1. **Banks and insurance companies should use more of the diverse and innovative pricing opportunities available to them.**
   As shown above, companies such as Microsoft, Dell and McDonalds have successfully used price differentiation because it offers huge potential for profit increase. Financial services

institutions should recognize the fact that their customers may have different preferences and requirements, and should develop more needs-based and segment-specific bundled products and price them using the innovative concepts outlined in this section.

2. **Managers should use a solid information basis and professional pricing methods.**

    Viable price strategies are dependent on reliable market and cost data. While cost data may be relatively easily obtained from within the financial institution, obtaining market data (e.g. price elasticity and utility values for different product features) requires considerable investment in primary research. Financial services institutions should use the professional methods described above to obtain insight on customer utility values and willingness-to-pay. These have proven to be a solid basis for professional pricing (see Chapter 4). Global financial services institutions should also consider using price corridors for products targeting globally active customers.

3. **Price differentiation: differentiate prices, however ensure that new pricing concepts are fully understood by both customers and sales people alike.**

    The implementation of a new pricing system for Germany's Deutsche Bahn is a good case study of how important this concept is to the success of any new price structure. The idea behind the price system (i.e. to differentiate prices based on capacity utilization, similar to the airline industry) was good, but its implementation was far too complex and faced harsh criticism from customers. Moreover, customer services staff did not understand the new system and found it difficult to communicate the new prices to customers. In the end, the pricing system had to be changed and re-launched before it was successfully accepted in the market. The lesson for the financial services industry is that given the complexity of most financial services products, it is even more important that their pricing and customer value proposition is simple and clearly communicated to both customers and sales teams.

4. **Managers should regularly examine new price and product concepts.**

    In light of ever changing market environments, there is a need to regularly check and, if necessary, adjust pricing concepts. However, financial services institutions need to find a balance and should avoid confusing customers with frequent changes to service offerings and pricing strategies. Financial services institutions should develop and enforce systematic price and product development processes (information gathering, rules and responsibilities of price decision making).

5.   **Financial services institutions need to communicate product and price concepts clearly and consistently to their customers.**

Market-oriented, intelligent product and pricing concepts are only effective if products are clearly communicated and understood by customers. As simple as this may sound, in practice it can be surprisingly difficult.

Psychological Aspects of Pricing

Psychology and pricing

Customers' awareness of price levels and perception of their appeal play an important role in how price changes impact their buying behavior. Both the availability and quality of price information, such as current interest rates, and management fees as well as a provider's price image, can all help determine the relationship between price and purchase decisions. The image of a price (i.e. how it is perceived by customers) will have more of an influence on customers when they have limited knowledge of the product's actual price. Indeed, research shows that psychological effects can have a significant impact on sales volume, revenue and profit of financial services products.

GROWING SIGNIFICANCE OF PSYCHOLOGY IN PRICING

How customers react to a product's price largely depends on how they perceive and evaluate it. Hence, understanding how important price components are to customers is a key price management competence. The following example demonstrates this point more clearly: a typical checking account comprises a variety of price components, including account management fees, debit card fees, ATM fees, paper-based and online transaction fees and credit interest. Which of these price components do customers focus on when evaluating the price of a product, and which should be discounted? Both of these questions have important consequences for the communication of a product's price, and therefore on sales volume, revenue and profit. For this reason, financial services managers should familiarize themselves with the psychological aspects of pricing.

Pricing can be even more important in advertising financial services. Direct banks advertise an attractive interest rate on their savings accounts, and in so doing, position themselves as "price leaders" in that category. Other banks choose to offer a free checking account, and position themselves as "basic and simple". GEICO promotes "15 minutes can save you 15 percent or more" on car insurance to position itself as the price leader for car insurance in the US. The following topics illustrate the main effects of pricing psychology on financial services companies:

Price Awareness: many managers overestimate the level of price knowledge for their products and often assume the customer is equally well informed as they are. In reality, customers' price awareness of financial services products, in general, is surprisingly low. Managers' incorrect assumptions about awareness of prices often lead to incorrect pricing and marketing decisions.

Price Image: many banks and insurers underestimate the impact of price image. Customers often lack a high level price knowledge and price awareness. As a result, they rely heavily on providers' price images as an indicator of the actual price of their products. It is therefore imperative to maintain a desirable price image among target customer groups.

Price Perception: financial services products include so many individual price components that customers, and even advisors, often become confused. It is crucial to understand how different price components are perceived by customers, i.e. how much customers focus on prices and which price levels they perceive as "low", "high", and "fair".

Price Thresholds: price thresholds are, to a large extent, overlooked by financial services institutions. Their relevance and potential impact on customers' purchasing decisions is usually unknown. Managers are just now beginning to understand the importance of price thresholds.

While many institutions remain conservative, others have adopted a technique widely used in consumer retail companies, experimenting with prices set just below a threshold value (e.g. $9.99 rather than $10.00).

Management of price awareness, price image and price perception

The following frameworks provide valuable price management recommendations with regard to the psychological aspects of pricing.

PRICE AWARENESS: HOW WELL DO CUSTOMERS KNOW THE PRICE OF A PRODUCT/SERVICE?

The mere breadth of an institution's product range often prevents customers from knowing the prices of certain products. Figure 6.1 shows the results of a recent study on the awareness of account maintenance fees.

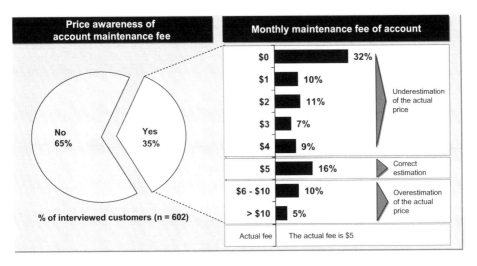

Figure 6.1   Price awareness of account maintenance fee components

Even though the checking account is the most standard retail banking product, 65 percent of the customers interviewed said they had no knowledge of the fees they were being charged. In fact, of the 35 percent that believed they did know the fee, only 16 percent were correct. As a percentage of the entire population of participants, only 6 percent were aware of the correct price (69 percent underestimated and 15 percent overestimated the price). Similarly, with other price components, such as deposit interest or deposit fees, customers were scarcely aware of the correct price.

Similar results can be seen in other product areas (see Figure 6.2). While more than half of the respondents believed they were aware of the price for their debit (51 percent) and credit card (56 percent), only 31 percent could call to mind the deposit fee. In the end, most of the customers overestimated every price component, and only 5–15 percent accurately estimated the correct rates and fees.

The results of the study showed that overall price awareness of financial services products among customers is low. It follows that "price aggressive" companies should emphasize their products' price advantages relative to competing products. In contrast, "price defensive" and established financial services institutions may want to take advantage of their customers' low price awareness. First, a systematic analysis of customer price awareness will reveal the extent to which individual price components can be increased and the amount of additional profit that would result from the price change. Secondly, in order to position the bank as attractive on price, tactical discounting of highly visible price components should be considered.

Price awareness of selected banking products		
Selected products	% of interviewees who thought they knew the price	% of interviewees who knew the actual price
Deposit fee	31%	5%
Checking account	35%	6%
Deposit interest rates	41%	11%
Debit cards	51%	13%
Credit cards	56%	15%

Figure 6.2   Price awareness of selected banking products

Customer price awareness is especially important in multi-dimensional pricing. When the price quoted for a given product depends on certain customer criteria, it is very difficult for the customer to determine in advance what he is likely to pay. Financial services companies frequently benefit from this by advertising the lowest possible price and attracting new customers who perceive the product to be a good value. In the end, the price paid by customers can, depending on the customer's profile, significantly differ from the originally promoted price.

PRICE IMAGE: BUILDING A POSITIVE PRICE IMAGE

Customers, unaware of prices or overwhelmed by the shear quantity of price components, will often base their decision to switch financial services providers on their opinion of a provider's price image. "Price image" in this context refers to the impression customers have of a company with respect to its prices. Competing hypotheses offer two approaches to creating a price image. Within the context of financial services, they are:

Hypothesis 1: customers create a price image based on their perception of only a small number of prices, especially those of key products, special offers and advertised products.

Hypothesis 2: customers create a price image based on their personal level of consumption and usage, and hence, their price image incorporates a larger number of financial services products – all the products they have personal experience with.

These hypotheses, widely confirmed in many retail customer studies, suggest that, once established, changing a price image is extremely difficult.

Hence, building a "value for money" and "fair price" image has significant advantages. Many incumbent financial institutions, including established banks and insurance companies, often carry a relatively expensive price image. In this case, their goal should be to improve the price image of key products. There is often enormous room to use intelligent forms of price differentiation to achieve superior price images.

If price image is determined by a small number of core products or by special offers (hypothesis 1), then selective product discounting is recommended to improve the appearance of these products relative to the competition ("window dressing approach"). This strategy requires heavy marketing of the discounted products to position them, and the desired image, at the forefront of customers' awareness.

PRICE PERCEPTION: HOW DO CUSTOMERS PERCEIVE PRICE INFORMATION?

The term price perception describes the mental recognition and processing of price information. The complexity of price perception rises in line with the amount of product and price combinations offered; analysis shows that there are more than 350 price components in an average product portfolio of a financial services institution. This poses the question, how do customers perceive price information?

In a typical example, a corporate bank offers four alternative account options comprising many price and service components. There are seven separate price components in each of the bundles (basic price, discount, prices for debit and credit cards, prices for paper-based and online transactions and prices for monthly standing orders). Management wondered what impact price information has on customers' price perception, their evaluation of the individual price components and the bundle price, and, finally, their willingness-to-pay. In order to make pricing decisions, such as determining discounts levels, management felt it crucial to know which product and price components in the bundle would receive the most customer attention. The following case studies highlight some real-life examples of financial services companies in similar situations and how they dealt with psychological pricing topics:

Case study 1: checking account packages in retail banking

A major UK financial services provider had the challenge of designing a new checking account package. Management was unsure how customers perceived the various price and product components (such as the account maintenance fee and interest rates). The strategic goal was to design a product that would influence customers to perceive the products and services as "value for money", or at the very least "fair".

A computer aided survey was used to assess customers' product preferences, price perceptions and price sensitivity. The results were supplemented with additional insight from an expert judgment survey and internal data analysis. The combination of all relevant data indicated that a strong price perception highly correlated to a high price elasticity of the product components. The revenue–risk matrix in Figure 6.2 shows the resulting customer price sensitivities and revenue impact.

The sensitivity analysis suggested that customers had a low perception of the paid referral fee (component 2) and interest rates on unauthorized overdrafts (component 10). Hence, the financial services provider increased the price of both components, with the OFT's (The Office of Fair Trading: UK's consumer regulatory body) concerns regarding the level of paid referral fees in mind. On the other hand, the interest rates on authorized overdrafts (component 5) were reduced, since the component was the focus of a marketing effort and customers were highly aware of it. In all, the institution's adoption of price differentiation based on customers' price perception led to a substantial increase in annual profits.

Case study 2: price perception in fund management

A fund management company's pricing structure consisted of four price components: a front-end load of 5 percent, a management fee of 1.5 percent per

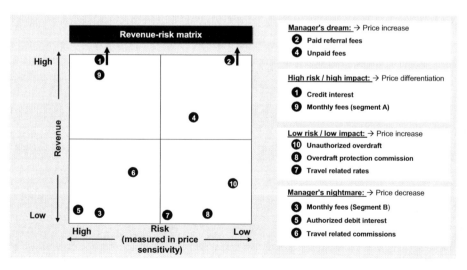

Figure 6.3   Application of the revenue-risk matrix

year, an account service fee of $350 per year, and a back-end load of 5 percent (as an alternative to front-end load). The management team wanted to know how different price components influenced their customers' price perception.

Conjoint measurement was used to measure the relative importance of the four price components. The analyzed price range of the respective components was +/- 25 basis points of the current level. Figure 6.4 compares the average perceived level of importance of the price components for a fund investment of $100,000 with the actual share of annual costs allocated to each component (Time period: five years).

The research delivered valuable insights for price management. Namely, that the relative importance of the front-end load in customer purchasing decisions was nearly double that of its share of costs (25 percent versus 43 percent). Customers appeared to focus on this price component more than it seemingly deserved. In contrast, the management fee, with 37 percent of total costs, was nearly twice as important (21 percent) as customers perceived it to be. In other words, customers perceived the management fee to be less important than the portion of cost it actually represented.

Such insights are very significant for price design. In the above case, management decided to reduce the front-end load and de-emphasize the management fee in its marketing communication. The message to take away is that in order to increase customers' awareness and create a positive impression

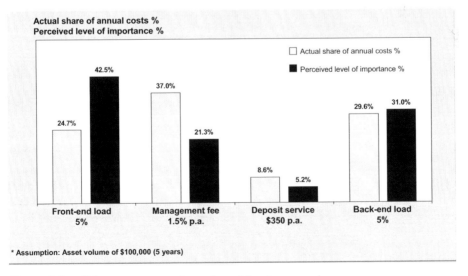

Figure 6.4   Price awareness: investment funds example

of their overall offering, providers should discount those price components that are perceived by customers to be most important. Many fund managers have already applied this method, and thereby increased their customers' willingness to buy their products. Fidelity Investments, for example, has tried to enter new markets by aggressively pricing and marketing low front-end loads.

Case study 3: new pricing structure in the securities advisory sector

Mergers are often an opportunity to re-align and make disparate pricing models consistent. In one instance, a financial services institution with a focus on retail securities trading merged with an institution focused on securities trading for high net worth customers, two segments with very different behaviour patterns. The integration required a merger of antiquated pricing structures into one which offered enough flexibility to cater to the needs of the banks disparate customer segments.

The new pricing model was made up of three price schemes, much in the same way as mobile phone fee structures. Scheme A had a low asset-based fee but a higher transaction fee, and scheme C had a lower transaction fee but a higher asset-based fee. Scheme B offered a blend of the two. Hence, the three schemes were positioned along a scale from "pay per use" to "flat fee". The new structure offered customers the ability to choose an appropriate mix of prices that fit their own expected use. Customers not intending to trade heavily opted for scheme A, whereas heavier traders opted for scheme C.

The price levels were again set with the help of a conjoint methodology, used to calculate the price elasticities of the most important price components. Customers who chose scheme A focused mostly on minimum prices (e.g. asset-based fee and account services fees). Hence, for scheme A, the provider undercut the competition on these prices, whereas prices were slightly increased for those components that were less important to customers. Prices for transaction fees and commission rates were of greater importance to customers who preferred scheme C. Again, this preference was taken into account when changing the price levels. The successful introduction of this new pricing model resulted in an 8 percent increase in profits.

Another important aspect influencing customer price perception is the notion of payment frequency. One aspect of frequency is the time period for which a price is communicated. A car insurance premium, for example, can refer to a month, quarter or year ($468 per year versus $39 per month). Frequency can also refer to the rate at which fees are paid. Monthly payment periods are frequent in financial services, even when prices are quoted on an annual basis (quarterly and yearly payment periods are common as well). Both types of frequency can have a significant impact on customers' price perception. The decision on both the time period a price refers to and the payment frequency depend not only on the product or service, but also on the customer segment and the company's technical capabilities.

Price thresholds

Price thresholds are price points which, when exceeded, have a significant impact (either positive or negative) on sales volume. This is a widely recognized phenomenon. In consumer retailing, in particular, prices are frequently set just below a recognized price threshold (e.g. $9.99), and financial services managers are similarly using price thresholds more frequently. Arguments in favor of utilizing price thresholds include:

- Consumers break prices down into discrete subcategories. For example, the price $3.99 is registered as belonging to the "under $4 category".

- Consumers perceive a savings compared to the round number.

- Consumers underestimate prices that lie just below a threshold.

- The first digit of a price influences consumers' price perception the most. Hence a price of $4.90 is perceived as "$4 plus". Moreover, consumers tend to perceive the digits of a price from left to right with reducing intensity.

The key message here is that managers in the financial services industry should dedicate more of their time to understanding the nature of price thresholds. As the following case demonstrates, intelligent price management strategies that utilize price thresholds can have a significant impact on an institution's revenues and profits.

CASE STUDY 4: PRICE THRESHOLDS IN SAVINGS ACCOUNTS

A financial services institution was put under competitive pressure by an aggressive offer of an online direct bank with an interest rate of 2.0 percent which was, at that time, significantly above the market average. The impact on the bank was:

- Significant outflow of funds.

- Perceived lack of offering targeted to price sensitive customers.

- Growing customer dissatisfaction with the lack of product alternatives.

As a result, senior management wanted to explore potential counter measures for offering its own attractive online account. With the exact level of the interest rate still to be decided, there were two alternative opinions to explore. Although some executives believed the new rate should lie in the 2 percent range, others believed that it should be at least 2.5 percent. In order to solve this problem, a decision support model was created. It combined market and internal company data with empirically collected data on price elasticities. The latter were determined in a workshop held with internal experts. In the workshop, the participants were requested to estimate how changes in the interest rate would impact the inflow of funds. Using this data, a price-response function was derived (see Figure 6.5). This was then combined with other data, including internal costs, and translated into a profit function.

The results were quite surprising to say the least. The company found that interest rate changes of 50 bps up or down would have very little impact on the inflow of funds. Indeed, there would be little impact on profit as a result of interest rate changes within this range. However, increasing the rate to 3 percent would not only lead to a considerably higher inflow of funds, it would also generate far greater profits. Customer interviews confirmed the existence of this price threshold, and, on the basis of all the analyses, the company introduced an online savings account with an interest rate of 3 percent. As expected, it led to significant inflow of funds. Moreover, profits increased and customers benefited from the attractive rate.

Is the principle of price thresholds applicable to other financial services products? Is it reasonable to assume that pricing below price thresholds in the financial services industry positively impacts the purchasing behavior of customers and leads to an increase in sales volumes? These questions were

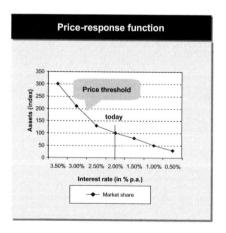
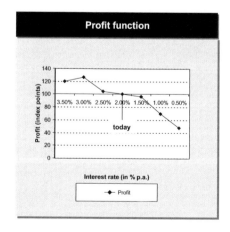

Figure 6.5   Price-response and profit functions

explored in a customer survey that had respondents choose between different products and price alternatives. The survey design placed the respondents into two groups, and although both groups evaluated the same products, the prices were set at different levels. Thus the approach enabled the psychological effect of the price threshold to be isolated and objectively measured.

The results of the survey showed that when a price is set below a known threshold, revenues will be 6 percent higher on average than revenues generated when prices are set on the price threshold itself. However, this revenue effect is largely dependent on the product type. Highly demanded products with which consumers have many provider options and can easily switch (such as credit cards) are more likely to benefit from price thresholds than products with a stronger "lock-in factor" (such as checking accounts). Overall, however, price thresholds are beginning to play a more important role in financial services price management and strategy.

Conclusion

- Consumers are not perfectly informed. Information asymmetries are particularly prevalent in financial services, making consumer price awareness and perception often as important as the actual price itself.

- It is vital that managers fully consider psychological price effects because how a customer reacts to a price often depends on how they perceive and evaluate it. In turn, these reactions have a significant impact on sales volume, revenue and profit. It is vital that managers do not underestimate the impact of price image.

- Price thresholds are a particularly good example of psychological price effects that carry a significant impact. Thresholds are price points which, when exceeded, have a significant (negative or positive) impact on sales volume. Managers should dedicate more time to setting price points below these thresholds as the revenue and profit potential is significant and the risk of lost revenue and profit is extremely low.

- The growing recognition of the importance of pricing psychology and price awareness is evident in the move towards flat rates, price bundling, and the increased focus on price in financial services advertising.

Price Implementation Issues

CHAPTER

7

Implementation and pricing

In the previous chapters, the methods and concepts of price optimization for financial products and services were described. However, in order to profit from improved pricing, it is vital to address numerous implementation issues. What follows are the organizational prerequisites for ensuring that pricing is managed properly. This chapter focuses on how to optimally organize pricing structures and processes, develop price information systems, and improve the implementation of prices in the marketplace.

Pricing organization

In many financial services institutions pricing is not managed professionally. In contrast to the pharmaceutical and automotive industries, pricing often has no organizational home or dedicated management role, such as "Head of Pricing". The previous chapters emphasized the importance of professional pricing for financial services institutions and proposed that managers take a critical look at price management within their company. Price management should be integrated into the organization in such a way that products are correctly and efficiently priced for all customer segments. Pricing guidelines based on corporate strategy form the basis for setting segment-specific pricing strategies and goals. Figure 7.1 represents a conceptual framework for creating an efficient pricing organization to implement such strategies.

Common pricing issues, such as a lack of pricing strategy or non-systematic discount management, should be resolved by the pricing organization in a consistent manner. When establishing a pricing organization, the following questions should be answered:

- Who is responsible for determining prices for banking, investment, and insurance products?

- Who awards discounts, in what form, and to what extent?

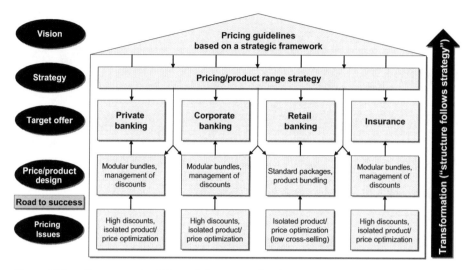

Figure 7.1   Framework of the pricing organization

- How are different organizational functions (marketing, finance or sales) coordinated when it comes to pricing?

- Where should the price management function be located within the organization?

- What information is needed to make educated pricing decisions? How should the necessary data be managed?

The fundamental responsibility of a pricing team within a financial services institution is to ensure that each task of the pricing process is systematically and consistently carried out. The pricing team has to be an integral part of the organization as a whole.

The way the pricing team and its responsibilities are structured should follow the principle of "structure follows strategy". Harvard Professor Alfred Chandler used these words in 1962 to describe the results of his empirical research on the relationship between strategy and organizational structure. He concluded that strategy determines an organization's structure. Decisions made as part of a pricing strategy, which are developed into strategic goals and pricing principles, are not only drivers of subsequent stages of the pricing process (e.g. pricing analysis and setting), but are also the basis for positioning the pricing function within the organization.

Research by Simon-Kucher and Partners in the financial services sector has shown that the "structure follows strategy" principle is frequently ignored. In the vast majority of institutions, pricing across diverse product areas is managed independently, and, as a result, individual pricing managers do not see the "big picture" and are ill-equipped to deal with all relevant information at once. The following quotes by financial services executives underscore this:

- "In our bank there are hardly any offerings that span different product areas. Therefore, cross-selling does not work".

- "There is not enough coordination between different areas on product and price optimization".

- "Each product area develops its own pricing concepts. Often, one area knows nothing about the other's work".

Pricing often has no home in the organization, nor do systematic processes to coordinate individual pricing activities exist to reflect the institution's corporate strategy.

Many managers see pricing as an auxiliary activity rather than a fundamental part of business success. Pricing activities in financial services institutions are normally ad hoc and uncoordinated while other industries remain far more advanced. For example, Akzo Nobel, a chemical manufacturer, established its own dedicated pricing department with specialists who periodically carry out critical pricing checks within the industry and regularly monitor how well the company's pricing strategy is adhered to. The automotive, airline and travel industries have all recognized that pricing can only be properly and consistently addressed if it has a permanent home within the organization. This is rarely the case in the financial services industry. UBS has, for example, created a function called the "Pricing Manager", but most banks have not.

Three conditions are critical for the optimal execution of pricing responsibilities within an organization:

1. A multitude of different resources must be coordinated in the price management process. This includes, among others, marketing, sales, product development, product management, finance and IT.

2. Since pricing has a direct and significant effect on profit, senior management needs to be closely involved, especially as they have the capability to pool all necessary resources within the company.

3. Pricing structures and processes must be flexible enough to be effective in all major business areas of the company.

The large number of potential pricing related issues means that it is not possible to estimate the number of representatives needed from each functional area. For instance, the challenges of optimizing rates for commercial loans (risk management, Basel II, integration of market and cost information) are different from those of pricing retail checking accounts. By accumulating knowledge within the organization, however, it is possible to generate efficiencies in pricing processes.

Senior management involvement in the process is essential for building an effective pricing function, but it is not enough. Pricing needs an operational home with a dedicated manager coordinating the pricing process. Two types of pricing organizational structures exist: dedicated pricing departments, and panels from different functional areas of the organization who take on pricing issues as they emerge. Dedicated pricing groups, however, come at a higher fixed cost and offer less flexibility than utlizing existing resources.

Therefore, the optimal configuration of a pricing organization in many cases is the following: besides creating a "Head of Pricing" function, a "Pricing Board" should be established, consisting of members of the senior management team as well as specialists from the IT, marketing, and finance departments chosen to devote time to the pricing effort. This structure should be complemented with external competencies such as specialized business consultancies as required.

The Head of Pricing coordinates all pricing related activities within the company. They report to the senior management team and manage the technical and operational aspects of the pricing board. Specifically, they have the following responsibilities:

1. Overseeing the quality of all price-relevant information (such as cost, revenue and sales volume).

2. Defining pricing-related tasks for IT, finance and marketing.

3. Carrying out customer surveys on willingness-to-pay, price elasticity and price-response functions.

4. Regular analysis of the price structure and pricing levels in place, and development of specific actions to improve them.

5. Monitoring pricing of newly introduced products based on their price–value relationship, and working across departments to conceptualize new products.

6. Assessing the price consistency across the entire company based on the corporate pricing strategy.

7.   Regularly controlling the granting of discounts by sales (advisors) and installing early warning systems.

8.   Regularly conducting performance analyses with respect to the metrics dictated by the corporate strategy (sales volumes, prices, profit).

9.   Carrying out all defined pricing management and coordination functions within the company.

The progress of pricing activities should be monitored on a regular basis and any new measures must be agreed upon and initiated by the pricing board. Under the supervision of the Head of Pricing, the pricing board should regularly convene to address pricing issues. To integrate as much expertise as possible, representatives from cross-divisional functions, such as IT and finance, relevant pricing specialists, as well as external experts, should all be involved in these pricing deliberations. The Head of Pricing should over time gain an overview of the market and become aware of the specific competencies of his or her team, and thus be responsible for coordinating their involvement in pricing activities. It is essential for the development of the pricing organization that the responsibilities of the pricing board members be clearly defined. The example in Figure 7.2 shows the typical division of price management tasks for a banking product.

Finally, Figure 7.3 shows a job description for a role equivalent to that of the Head of Pricing.

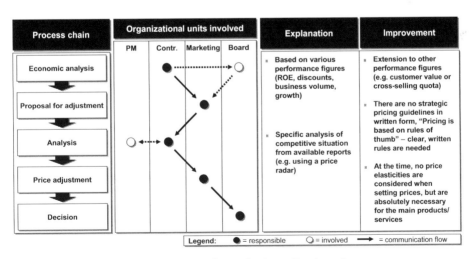

Figure 7.2   Example of a process flow of price adjustments

Senior Cost & Pricing Manager

Location: Washington DC
Salary: TBD
Company: XXXXXX
Job type: Permanent
Date posted: 04/21/2008
Description: *Senior Cost & Pricing Manager*

Summary: This division is involved in the entire pricing procedure any time a new project is bid with an expected total value over $100,000. Candidate must have the contacts and resources to help resolve pricing issues when they arise.

Position Summary: The Senior Cost and Pricing Manager will be responsible for the complete development of complex financial proposals ... The individual must have strong product development skills as well as actual prior experience in developing and pricing proposal budgets.

Essential Job Functions:
- Review and analysis of the financial requirements of a solicitation and work with the technical team and officer-in-charge in the development of questions to the client, changes to the cost proposal and in developing a strategic approach to pricing the project;
- Develop entire response to simple and complex business proposals in compliance with the funding firm's pricing requirements and format.
- Demonstrated ability to work closely with the technical proposal team and officers-in-charge in the development of various types of proposals and with various types of funding sources;
- Analysis of different types of data in order to provide strategic guidance;
- Negotiate salaries, budgets, and other cost matters with clients, subcontractors, consultants, and proposed project staff;
- Review of proposed contracts, subcontracts, or agreements for accuracy and compliance issues as well as develop and negotiate changes to proposed language when necessary.

Specific Knowledge Requirements:
- Masters required or equivalent combination of education and work experience;
- 7 years of relevant experience required;
- Experience in cost proposal development;
- Experience in financial analysis; and
- Experience in contract negotiations services with firm(s) involved in the provision of pricing services

Figure 7.3   Job description for a pricing manager

(*Source*: Internet job site)

Price information systems

INCREASING IMPORTANCE OF PRICE INFORMATION SYSTEMS

Despite having a vast amount of information on the behavior of their customers, banks and insurers are increasingly faced with a lack of data and transparency of their current pricing practices. This is where price information systems (PIS) can be useful. They provide meaningful pricing data, help produce management level pricing reports, and form the basis for professional price optimization. PIS make current pricing practices more transparent, and thus help management to make fact-based pricing decisions in a focused and efficient manner. Ultimately, this should lead to an increase in profit, greater customer satisfaction and improved customer relationships. "Pricing information systems will be very important for us in the future as they help improve the way we implement prices", a senior manager of a large global financial services institution recently said.

The basis for making pricing decisions – clarity and transparency of current pricing practices – often appears to be beyond a bank or insurers reach. Questions such as "how many and which customers pay the minimum price for deposit fees?", "how many customers are granted discounts for fixed-term deposits and to what extent?", or "how do the prices requested by customers differ from current list prices?" can often not be precisely answered by managers. Since the availability of data is uncertain, decisions are either made after long drawn out research, or the wrong decisions are made. A study carried out by *Business Week* (Basis: 700 managers questioned) showed that:

- Almost 80 percent of managers admit to having made wrong or sub-optimal decisions due to incomplete information or a lack of information altogether.

- Two thirds of managers are forced to make intuitive decisions based on insufficient information.

- A large number of managers complain that routine decisions, which only marginally contribute to performance, take increasing amounts of time due to a lack of data or the difficulty of accessing data.

Decisions made intuitively are not fundamentally bad. However, compared to other industries, pricing in the financial services sector has the following characteristics, which make it very difficult, if not impossible, to rely on merely intuitive estimations of price measure effects:

1. Numerous price and performance parameters: in most cases, price lists for financial services institutions contain several hundred price and component parameters, including fixed and usage-dependent prices. This also includes "indirect" pricing components such as pricing tiers, qualification criteria, individually negotiated agreements and "special" services.

2. Number of products (cross-selling): in addition to the individual price, the total fee the customer pays to the institution is important Therefore, pricing measures in one area impact price maneuverability in other product areas. Methods such as bundling or discount systems for products that span multiple categories can enable managers to increase their cross-selling potential. Financial

services institutions should be organized in such a way that their various functions appear integrated to the customer, even if pricing measures are undertaken by separated divisions.

3. Multi-person pricing: the combined assets of a group of people influence pricing and product policies and thus must be considered in price enforcement policies. For instance, well-off parents often demand similar terms and conditions for their children – it is the total level of assets for the "group" that determines pricing, rather than the individual assets of each member.

Given the sheer number of pricing parameters, the multitude of products and services, not to mention the nature of the client advisor relationship, producing a financial services pricing database is an extremely complex task, involving a significant amount of inputs. Figure 7.4 shows a typical database set up. Since the data was compiled from seven autonomous IT systems developed over time internally by the institution, integrating all the data points was time consuming and required significant involvement from the IT and finance teams.

In summary, price information systems can significantly help improve particular phases of the pricing process, especially the analysis stage (gaining transparency on price enforcement) and the monitoring/controlling phase. The systems provide pricing managers with the necessary information to make clear and confident decisions.

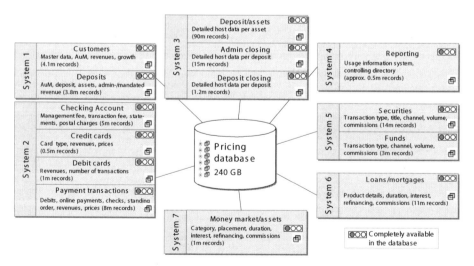

Figure 7.4   Structure of a comprehensive pricing database

EXAMPLES OF PRICE INFORMATION SYSTEMS

Below are two examples of price information systems used in the financial services industry.

A. Securities business in private banking

The private banking practice of a global financial services institution recognized that by offering differentiated prices and services to different customer groups, profits could be effectively increased. Secondly, it became apparent that the bank's securities business had no transparency over its price enforcement (i.e. actual versus target prices) and the various types of discounts granted. The aim of a pricing initiative was to create transparency on an individual customer level using a comprehensive, fully automated database, and to replace the current product/price landscape with a new needs-based pricing structure. Management wanted to understand how changing prices or price structures would affect sales volume, revenue and profit. With this in mind, a price information system was developed (see Figure 7.5).

A core component of the price information system was a set of databases containing individual customer portfolio and transaction data. The prices for the various services could be adjusted from a customized user interface. This enabled, among other things, an increased understanding of the impact of different pricing measures on revenue and profit as well as creating a so-called "win/loss" report (i.e. how individual customers or segments were affected by changes in price).

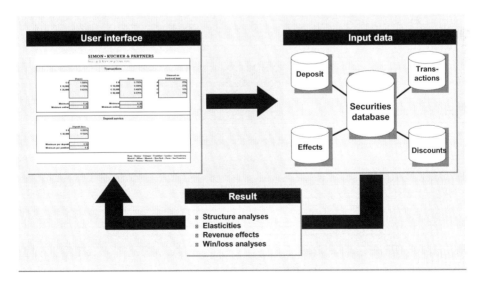

Figure 7.5   Structure of a price information system

With the new price information system the bank benefited twofold:

1.   **Transparency through structural analysis:** using the databases, management was able to carry out important structural analyses on existing data and calculate target revenues for various products and services based on list prices. The databases also contained the actual realized revenue. Comparing the target versus actual revenues enabled management to determine the level of discounts granted. For the first time, this important information became transparent. Figure 7.6 shows an example of the structural analysis of a complex price system for securities accounts. Approximately 84 percent of customer portfolio holdings were domestic securities handled by Euroclear, of which around two thirds had such a low overall value that the minimum price of €5 applied. The largest portion of revenue (48 percent) was generated by the lowest level of commission fee (0.22 percent). These findings had immediate implications for the price management of the financial services provider. For example, significant increases in revenue could only be achieved by raising the price for domestic securities traded through Euroclear. Reducing the other prices would not be effective, but could be useful for communications.

2.   **Optimization of the price structures:** the optimization of price levels was carried out using a simulation whereby each price was both raised and lowered within a particular range. This enabled quantifying the effect of changes in individual price components on the overall sales volume. Using a computer-aided customer

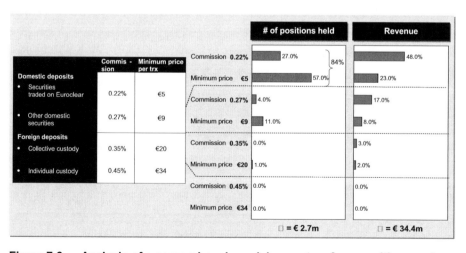

Figure 7.6   Analysis of a comprehensive pricing system for securities services

questionnaire (including conjoint measurement), information on individual customers' price sensitivities was gathered, enabling the price management team to directly identify revenue potential. In general, increasing prices for products with low price sensitivities, for example securities accounts, led to considerable revenue growth. The results of the survey indicated that the financial services institution could implement these changes with low risk. Customers reacted more strongly to an increase in the minimum price for transactions. The reason for this is that this price is at the forefront of the customer's perception. Even marginal changes in this price, which would only generate moderate revenues for the company, led to clear negative customer reaction. Management subsequently simulated combinations of price changes and calculated their cumulative effect on revenue. These calculations were made for each individual customer to produce win/loss statistics. Management used this analysis to establish appropriate pricing measures and to introduce a needs-based pricing model. Then it became possible to find precise answers to questions such as "what happens when a price per holding is introduced for the securities account?", "by how much does revenue increase, how many customers are affected by this?", or "what are the effects of differentiating price for different services?" The database covered around 25 million data records. The increase in revenue resulting from the implementation of the system was around 5 percent, around €30 million, and the level of customer attrition was minimal. Once created, this model formed the basis for future price decisions.

B. Business banking

Optimized price and discount structures are the foundation for efficient pricing in business banking. Therefore, this project focused on two stages of the pricing process: price implementation and price monitoring. In cases where the effective management of discounts is the main lever for margin improvements, the value add of price information systems can be huge, as the following example of business loans demonstrates: a bank introduced a systematic price monitoring system as part of a new structure for granting discounts in its loan business. This included a quarterly pricing report and a pricing cockpit. On an aggregated level, the pricing report exposed the actual prices and discounts granted and grouped the data according to various criteria. This report was based on a pricing database which contained the most important parameters, such as credit volumes, duration, list conditions, actual conditions, and refinancing clauses for all credits within the considered timeframe. Figure 7.7 below is an extract from such a pricing report, organized by region. The pricing cockpit enabled management to improve transparency of the interest rates and margins by drilling down into certain specific criteria within each region (e.g. analyzing margins by product, customer segment, branch or advisor).

Part A of Figure 7.7 shows the realized average interest rates in the individual regions. The difference in price implementation between individual regions of 0.37 percent points is relatively high (minimum Alsace: 4.17 percent; maximum Languedoc-Roussillon: 4.54 percent). Analyzing the causes of these differences showed that this could be partially explained by regional differences, i.e. the different competitive situation or diverse socio-demographics within the customer base. But there had to be other reasons too. To explore this, the high level results were broken down. Part B of Figure 7.7 is an example of such a detailed breakdown for realized credit rates of a selected type and duration by individual advisors in the Aquitaine region. It was clear that the varying performance of sales staff was causing the variation in price enforcement. Based on these findings, the following measures were implemented to improve price enforcement by the sales team:

- Creation of selling arguments and FAQs to improve the implementation of prices in the negotiation process.

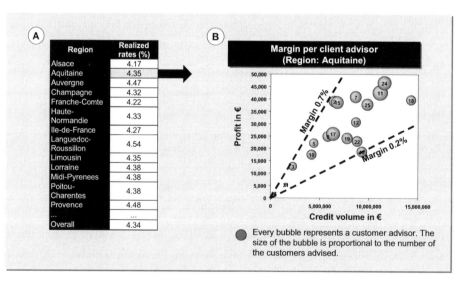

Figure 7.7   Extract from a pricing report

- Creation of a checklist to help the advisor to estimate the price sensitivity of customers.

- Systematic coaching by the top 20 advisors on current best pricing practices (learn from the best).

On top of that, the pricing database described above made it possible to assess how pricing was being applied according to various criteria, and to carry out individual customer and client advisor analyses. A pricing cockpit was created to carry out detailed and individual customer analysis as well as to provide targeted support for sales. The cockpit also produced reports of branches/advisors with particularly low price enforcement levels which could then be used by management in regular feedback sessions. The user interface for such a pricing cockpit is shown in Figure 7.8.

In this specific case, the pricing database contained around 30,000 individual credit contracts. In the first year after the pricing information system was introduced, margins increased by around ten basis points, corresponding to an increase in profits of around €6 million. Further feedback loops and more training for the advisors could in the medium term potentially result in annual profit growth of around €10 million.

PROCESS FOR DEVELOPING A PRICE INFORMATION SYSTEM

The process for developing a price information system can be divided into three steps which are described in more detail below.

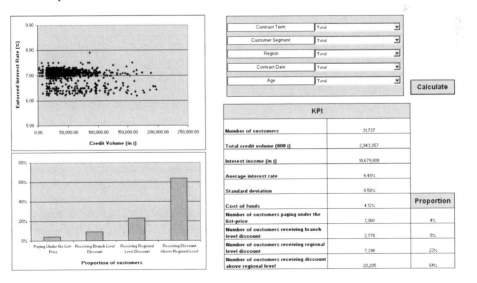

Figure 7.8   User interface of a pricing cockpit

1. Definition of the structure of a pricing database

First, the scope of the pricing database must be defined. The database must be built around the specific customer segment in question (a database for private customers will generally include different products than a database for commercial customers). Then, the products included must be defined. Initially only one product area is included, but in order to quantify the effect of cross-selling, efforts should be made to integrate all segment-specific products into the database in the medium term.

Then, internal experts should set parameters to describe the individual products. This should be done with care, as any improper decision can limit the future capabilities of the pricing database. If, for example, the intention is to differentiate the price for buying and selling securities in the brokerage sector according to time of day, the date and time of each trade must be included. Or, if the intention is to price counter transactions, the transactions database must include corresponding variables. It is essential for the analysis that the actual price paid as well as the list price for all the relevant products and services are included. The level of detail in the database is also very important: the more detailed the information, the more meaningful the results – although clearly a balance must be found between level of detail and size of database.

2. Integration of different databases

Most financial services institutions have a multitude of customer-specific information which, while very valuable, is often stored in different departments and systems (finance, operations and CRM). Even though it requires significant effort, all price-relevant data should be compiled in one single database. To structure the database optimally will naturally involve significant cooperation between departments, with the various data sets eventually being consolidated into a single pricing database.

Depending on the level of experience, this process can take anywhere between six to ten weeks, but once built, the database will enable finding and analyzing pricing information at a fraction of the time previously taken. The investment is worthwhile.

3. Developing reports and tools to optimize pricing and monitoring

Reports from the pricing database can be used by management to monitor and control performance against sales targets. Such reports should include only key performance indicators and be issued on a regular basis (e.g. monthly or quarterly). A pricing report on individual product areas should contain the following key data:

- Number of customers, revenue and assets under management per price model (for areas with differentiated price and product structures).

- Usage levels of individual products.

- Number of customers, who pay the list price and number of customers that are granted discounts, possibly sorted by customer segment, region, advisor or credit risk.

- Level and structure of the discounts granted.

- Cross-selling quotas.

The report is essential in order to monitor prices; however, developing other intelligent tools from the database information should also be considered. These tools could, for example, be used to configure account packages and optimize prices, reduce discounts, or even produce reports of customer discounts – all of which could be useful aids in discussions with sales teams.

Price implementation and sales incentive systems

Enforcing prices in the marketplace is the final step in the price implementation process. This section deals with the various aspects of price enforcement. This includes delegating pricing responsibilities, incentivizing sales teams, implementing price changes, and negotiating prices.

DELEGATION OF PRICING COMPETENCIES

In many areas (e.g. in private banking, corporate banking, or certain types of insurance), prices are negotiated on an individual basis between the customer and the advisor/relationship manager (RM). This raises the question as to what extent pricing responsibilities should be delegated to the relationship manager. There are arguments for and against giving RMs pricing responsibilities. In favor of delegation to the RM is the fact that due to face-to-face contact, they are best positioned to assess the customer's willingness-to-pay. The RM can react more flexibly and quickly to changes in the marketplace, and is, in most cases, more motivated when held accountable for pricing decisions. Generally, pricing issues surround the service level or product portfolio of a customer. If the advisor does not have sufficient pricing competencies and repeatedly needs to turn to head office for authorization, managing the overall customer relationship becomes more difficult. On the other hand, advisors are often too flexible during price negotiations, which suggests that delegating too much authority to RMs is a bad idea. "By now, around 60 percent of our new business is acquired through high discounts", says a manager of a global financial services institution. This can be explained by the increasing psychological pressure on the advisor[1] and the increasing price sensitivity of customers[2]. Head office is better geared to withstand this type of pressure. Centralizing price decisions, to a certain extent, helps avoid price inconsistencies between individual customers or segments. Figure 7.9 summarizes the main arguments for and against delegating pricing responsibilities to the advisor.

Simply put, there is no ideal solution. The optimal decision depends on individual circumstances. In our experience, we recommend caution when delegating pricing authority to the RMs. It is not advisable to give broad-reaching or full price authority to non-managers. In order to ensure that the RM still has enough flexibility when discussing prices with customers, we recommend giving a restricted amount of pricing authority in the form of clear rules for granting discounts (to whom and extent of discount). Also, the level of training and motivation of the RM, together with the corporate culture, strongly influence the way pricing responsibilities are delegated to advisors. The delegation of price responsibilities requires that the advisor

Figure 7.9   Arguments for and against delegation of pricing competencies

---

1   "Most customer advisors are fearful of price negotiations", according to a manager of a global insurance company.
2   "I don't want to pay any initial charge on my investment funds. If you don't meet me on price, I will change banks", is the typical threat used by many customers.

understands the consequences of his or her price decisions with respect to the achievement of the bank's goals (revenue, profit, customer satisfaction, etc.). This requires that advisors be trained on pricing issues before any sales negotiations take place.

Case study on the delegation of pricing responsibilities and the design of a discount granting processes

In many areas of financial services (for instance, private banking and commercial insurance) the pricing component that drives revenue and profit is not the list price but the realized price (i.e. list price minus discount). The level and form of any discount clearly has a significant impact on the profitability of a sale. The overall profitability of such products as mortgages, asset management, corporate insurance and fixed-term investments can be significantly affected by discounts. For these products, the list price is only an "anchor price"; normally, the discount level is what determines the margin. In this case study, the effective rates at different deposit levels of fixed-term deposits at a large financial services institution were analyzed (see Figure 7.10).

The result was alarming. Many deals were actually closed below the list price. There was no correlation between the net interest margin and the deposit level. The task, therefore, was to develop an optimal structure for discounts and rules for granting them (i.e. a structured discount allowance process). The new process for granting discounts is shown schematically in Figure 7.11.

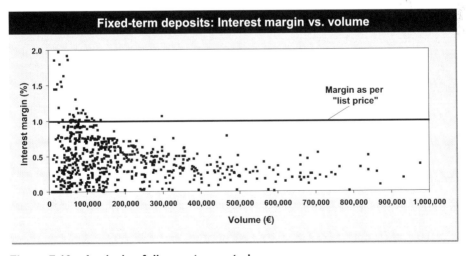

Figure 7.10 Analysis of discounts granted

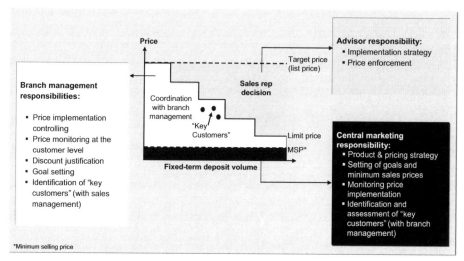

Figure 7.11   Structure and responsibilities of a discount allowance process

In addition to the list prices (target prices), the new system outlined "limit prices", which decrease with increasing customer investment (i.e. the volume invested in fixed-term deposits), and a minimum selling price (MSP). The salesperson (advisor) could set the price within these boundaries, but had to ensure that the lowest possible discounts were granted. This new discount structure was also supported by a corresponding change in the allowance process. Contracts below the limit price required branch manager authorization, and prices below the MSP required sales manager authorization. Only selected key customers were exempt from this rule. Such key customers could be customers using other products (e.g. mortgages and credits), or having high asset levels or belonging to a family account (e.g. the child of a family whose parents have significant assets).

Two years after this new system was introduced, the price discipline clearly improved. One success factor was a more stringent monthly price monitoring process that brought together members from product management and sales. This sharing of experiences significantly helped increase the sale staff's awareness of the effects of price on profit margins. Although the process of improving price discipline was difficult (in part because some assets were lost as customers left the bank), management was proved right in the end: income increased by more than 10 percent.

SALES INCENTIVIZATION

A key success factor in price implementation is setting the right incentives for sales teams. "Right" means that the structure of the incentive system, including optimal setting of incentive levels, has to be consistently aligned with the strategic pricing goals of the company. In practical terms this means that if senior management, for example, wants not only to increase volume and market share, but also to consistently increase profits and the number of new customers, then all these strategic goals need to be reflected in the sales team incentives. The process of developing such a pricing strategy-based sales incentive structure is shown in Figure 7.12.

Many financial services providers today do not use such a stringent process. This is particularly the case when attempting to increase profits through improved price implementation. The variable component of the advisor's commissions for securities business is often mostly linked to revenue (e.g. the volume of business from securities transactions) and partially to new business acquisition targets. The actual price at which individual transactions are made, after discounts the individual advisors has granted, is mostly not taken into account. As Figure 7.13 shows how this "price discipline" component can be built into the sales incentive system using a "price-implementation bonus".

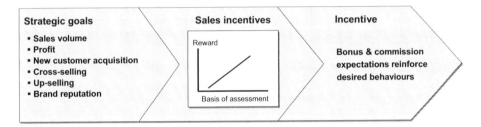

Figure 7.12   Process for a goal-based sales incentivization

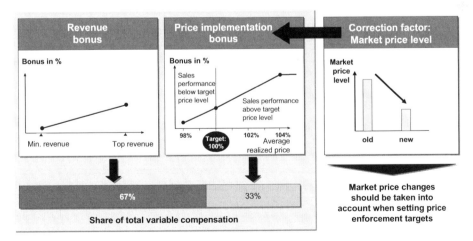

Figure 7.13   Example of a sales incentive system taking price enforcement into account

In this system, the revenue generated is the basis for calculating the commission for each advisor. The additional "price implementation bonus" explicitly rewards the advisor's price discipline by comparing his average realized price level with the target price level. An advisor who manages to generate high volumes and maintains a high level of price discipline is clearly a better price enforcer than a "notorious discount giver". Incorporating a relative performance measure (i.e. comparing the performance of each advisor to the average) will take market dynamics into account and provide constant performance improvement incentives. Additionally, through the correction factor, changes in market price levels during the course of the year can also be considered.

These types of systems, where sales incentives are based on the principle of price discipline, have already been successfully implemented in many financial institutions, and have contributed considerably to improved price implementation.

IMPLEMENTATION OF PRICE CHANGES

Generally, it is easier to enforce prices for new, innovative products than to increase prices on established financial products. This is especially true when:

- The new product is less comparable to established products.

- The new product fits better the into an established price-value position.

It is certainly difficult to gain customer acceptance for prices that are perceived as too high relative to the value delivered, but price acceptance is also low when new products with uncertain quality are introduced to the market. A well-known example is customers' resistance to pay for financial advice.

In today's dynamic markets, customer needs, competitive offerings and cost levels are constantly changing. Price adjustments are the necessary answers to these changes. Implementing price increases is certainly a major headache for many financial services institutions. Attempts to increase prices can often pit resistant customers and sales people against each other. A board member of a global insurance company posed the challenge in the following way: "If the decision has been taken to increase prices, then this must be consistently followed through".

In order to successfully implement higher prices, the following tips are helpful:

1.   Long term signaling: long before the date of any price change, management starts to talk about increased costs and the need to

raise prices. In this way, customers are gradually prepared and competitors are indirectly informed.

2. Timing: management chooses to time any price increase in such a way that the reason for a price rise appears particularly evident and credible, for example, following a central bank interest rate increase.

3. Increase in price with an accompanying change in service ("re-packaging"): a "cosmetic" change to the product accompanying the price increase can, at least partially, divert attention from price increase. This strategy is particularly successful for many retail banks when re-launching their checking account packages.

4. Number and increment of price increase: two moderate price increases influence the market less than one large jump in price. Management can claim that 'inflation' is causing costs to rise to justify this course of action.

5. Unbundling services: a bundled price (e.g. for a securities account package) can be separated into several price components (e.g. the base price for the account and trading fees), which are then set to a higher level, when summed, than the bundled price.

Being able to justify and communicate price changes plays an important role in any price increase situation, and experienced practitioners always point out the inherent danger of uprooting the trust between the advisor and customer in these situations. Price reductions are certainly the more pleasant side of price implementation, and the recommendations above can similarly be applied to price reductions. However, for customers who previously paid higher prices, price reductions can still sometimes be a source of irritation, and managers should consider any negative reaction before making *any* changes.

PRICE NEGOTIATIONS

Particularly in commercial and private banking, the final price of services is often determined through negotiation. The success of such negotiations depends on the level of understanding of pricing basics (such as the relationship between price, volume and revenues/profits), and on the tactical ability to negotiate.

Often, not enough attention is paid to training staff on pricing issues. Many advisors don't fully understand the effect of price changes on sales volume, revenue and profit. In the end, price implementation often very much depends on the personal interaction between customer and advisor. Below are ten tips that can be used by advisors in price negotiations, their relative importance and use, however, should be considered on a case-by-case basis.

1. Customer's willingness-to-pay depends on the perceived value of the product. Value (and not price) should be at the center of any negotiation.

2. Reduce the comparability of your products or services with competitors by incorporating additional services or through innovative price structures (e.g. bundling and non-linear pricing).

3. Make concessions on secondary items (such as giveaways) rather than on price.

4. Ask the customer to make more transactions, carry more assets with you, buy additional products, or recommend new customers in return for giving a discount.

5. Divide price concessions into stages. Instead of offering a 10 percent discount in one go, divide the discount into three or four stages.

6. If necessary, bundle financial products, ideally a "leader" product with a "filler" product. Only give in on the price of the stronger product if the customer also buys the "filler" product.

7. In practice, a conversation on price cannot be avoided; however, try to delay it until you have sufficiently communicated the value of your offering.

8. Consider that in price negotiations, it is not only about price and product, but also about person. Hence, concentrate on building a strong relationship with the customer.

9. Since the largest concessions are made due to time pressure, do not let yourself be put under time pressure when negotiating prices.

10. If you have no other choice, break the product down in order to achieve an acceptable price for the customer.

Case Studies

CHAPTER
8

Introduction

The following chapter provides a number of carefully chosen case studies drawn directly from the financial services industry. They illustrate what "price management" is and how it can be successfully applied.

CASE STUDIES

1. A new price model for payment systems.

2. Pricing strategies for foreign trade business.

3. Value-added checking account packages.

4. An innovative securities price model for private banking.

5. New securities price model in brokerage.

6. Intelligent price and growth model in private banking.

7. Price transparency and monitoring in retail banking.

8. Brand premium in corporate banking.

9. Smart pricing for investment funds.

10. Cost and needs-based packaged solutions in basic banking services.

11. Defining master pricing processes in retail and private banking.

12. Psychological aspects of pricing in private banking.

13. Cross-products loyalty pricing scheme in retail and private banking.

14. SEPA-conforming payment packages.

15. Price elasticity measurement for insurance businesses.

16.   Successful product differentiation based on customer value in motor insurance

A new price model for payment systems (B2B sector)

BACKGROUND AND GOALS

The landscape of the banking industry has undergone a period of fundamental change. The traditional value chain of the fully integrated universal bank has been undone. Non-core business processes are increasingly being outsourced to specialists, and competition among these specialists is becoming ever more intense.

The bank in this case study focused on handling payment transactions on behalf of other banks. Payment processing is a scale-driven business with unit costs diminishing at an increasing rate as more payments are processed. In order to strengthen its competitive edge, the transaction bank was planning to pass on its scale-based cost savings in the form of lower prices. However, without volume or performance incentives written into its contracts, the bank failed to explicitly reward those customers who were heavy users of the system and who made the system's cost structure viable. In addition, the bank's pricing process and the terms and conditions of its products and services were highly obscure. The complex price lists were not understood even by the most knowledgeable of the bank's customers. In this highly standardized business, a supplier can, however, counteract the pure price competition by offering its customers value-added additional services which it can deliver more efficiently than its competitors.

Against this background, three goals emerged for the transaction bank:

1.   To achieve maximum return on investment through applying a smart price reduction strategy. Overall price reductions across all customer segments should hardly be perceived by the bank's customers.

2.   To implement a transparent pricing structure because lower prices create a competitive advantage only when perceived by the customer. This should follow the quid-pro-quo principle: more volume leads to lower price per unit.

3.   To enhance the value proposition by offering more meaningful value-added services.

APPROACH

To gain transparency on the bank's performance, a database of internal data was set up. In almost every project we are involved in, our customers are positive that all the data needed is available at the click of a button. That is, however, a fallacy. In most cases, the necessary information is scattered in autonomous systems. Compiling the necessary data from often disparate IT environments within a bank and preparing it for analysis involves expenditures which are almost always underestimated.

While the database was being developed, a series of workshops were held with senior management, sales and selected customers. It is important to bring sales in at an early phase of pricing projects to ensure their buy-in as they are the ones to communicate price changes to the marketplace.

Customer involvement in the process not only provides first-hand knowledge, but also guarantees easier implementation in the market. For this reason, particular emphasis was put on including opinion leaders. Customer and competitor reaction to price changes was analyzed using the SKP-PriceStrat tool referred to in Chapter 4. This methodology uses the knowledge of internal experts who are involved in pricing to make recommendations based on price elasticity estimates.

All this information, in conjunction with data on the current state of the business, was then combined into a decision-support model to assess alternative pricing scenarios with respect to their effect on price, sales volume and profits. The model also made it possible to analyze the effect on an individual customer level. In addition, the value-added services conceptualized during the workshops with the opinion leaders were bundled optimally with the help of the decision-support model.

KEY FINDINGS

The structure of the new price model is shown in Figure 8.1. The complexity of the product alternatives was significantly reduced. By cleverly combining different products and prices into packages, the number of products was cut by around 30 percent. The new products had a clear pricing structure and equitable price levels.

The new price model was designed to incentivize usage of the payment system. The first step towards achieving this was offering a package of analytical services ("analysis package"), which provided customers with

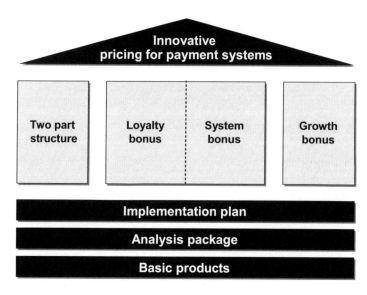

Figure 8.1   Innovative price model for payment systems

complete transparency on the current state of their business. Moreover, these analytics allowed the bank to identify the growth potential of each customer and enabled the formation of a strategic corporate growth plan (including implementation).

The core of the pricing itself is a two-part structure, comprising a fixed fee and a transaction fee. The fundamental idea is that each customer is free to choose the most appropriate combination of fixed and variable costs – the higher the fixed amount, the lower the transaction fee. This creates greater transparency by distinguishing between the transaction costs and the costs of supplementary services. In addition, this approach also takes into account the customer's own preferences: the fixed price provides stability that enables business planning, and the variable element offers flexibility. Lastly, this method of pricing follows the performance principle – the price for every customer is determined by his contribution to the system. Customers that input large volumes into the trading system realize economies of scale.

Due to the inherent scalability of the business, payment processors look to secure the greatest possible share of customer transactions. Therefore, the price model is designed to reward those customers who do not "cherry-pick", but put all their business through one system. The built in loyalty bonus compensates customers who use multiple services in a single area of business, while customers who are active in the greatest number of areas are rewarded with a system bonus. This benefits the bank by reducing "cherry-picking" and the gains from economies of scale are partially passed on to the customer. In addition, these gains of economies of scale should also be passed on to customers who grow their payment transactions. In order to reward high growth customers and to offer further growth incentives to all customers, an additional "growth bonus" was introduced which constituted a significant portion of the overall price reduction.

This new price model was the optimal price reduction strategy. Alternative price scenarios, which were simulated through the decision-support model, would have required triple the investment to achieve the same effect. Tens of millions of Euros savings were achieved.

In addition to the significant price reduction for the bank's most important customers, the new price model provided transparency (no hidden costs), simplicity (understandable bulk-purchasing, clear volume and performance incentives) and fairness (customers choose their own price; quid-pro-quo principle). Moreover, the supplementary services enabled above-average growth in the market share.

IMPLEMENTATION

The new price model was implemented in the marketplace through a two-pronged approach. The sales department underwent intensive training in the principles, key elements and trigger points of the new model, while the customers were familiarized with the benefits of the model.

In addition to numerous sales workshops, a detailed document was produced with FAQs on the new price model. This document included not only explanations on how the new model was constructed, but also arguments to be used in communication with customers. Each member of the sales team also received an analysis of the effects of the new system on each of their customers.

Informative sessions were arranged to familiarize the most important customers with the new model. The key tool in this process was a computer-based simulation model, which each member of the sales team could download on his laptop. This model made it possible to analyze the effects of the new price model in detail and to run different scenarios and quantify their impact. This approach allowed the sales team to guide their customers through the various options to grow their business with the bank and the necessary steps to reach their growth goals. The simulation tools were critical for the successful implementation of the new price concept in the marketplace.

Pricing strategies for foreign trade business (B2B sector)

BACKGROUND AND GOALS

Foreign trade occurs when companies trade goods and services across borders with foreign business partners. As banks are increasingly gearing themselves up to act as intermediaries between trading partners, direct contact between the contracting partners is not required to complete the financial side of a foreign trade deal. As a general rule, the larger the number of different financial instruments used in a business deal, the lower the risk for both companies. For example, while prepayment provides exporters with the most security, importers benefit most from deals with open payment terms. Financial institutions in the foreign trade market offer an extensive range of products, such as letters of credit or guarantees, which can accommodate the needs of both parties involved.

This business segment was proving to be unprofitable for the bank in this case study. The degree of individualization when tailoring financial instruments to customers' needs – often including an element of lending – requires a large number of personnel. In addition, due to highly complex products, specialists that draw relatively high salaries in comparison to the average compensation level at the bank are required.

The bank underwent a change in strategy. Previously, the foreign trade business had been cross-subsidized by other areas of the bank. The board of directors decided, however, that in the future the foreign trade business would need to be profitable as a stand alone entity.

Two principal goals were defined for the project:

- To investigate whether the current price levels left room for intelligent price increases.

- To analyze the current price structure for optimization. Originally, pricing was determined primarily by the amount of the underlying deal. The board requested that, in the future, price levels reflect costs incurred. Whether this principle could be implemented in a future price structure had to be investigated.

APPROACH

Using the SKP-PriceStrat methodology, pricing workshops were held with product and market experts. Participants were asked to evaluate how the volume of sales of individual products would change if the prices were lowered or increased. Each expert completed a questionnaire which was then evaluated and used in the workshop. Using the PriceStrat algorithm, price-response functions for selected products were estimated and discussed. The price-response function for each product was then transformed into a revenue function which could be used to analyze the economic effects of various pricing scenarios.

Simultaneously, workshops with product experts and selected customers were held to further define the characteristics of the products offered. In order to define a consistent pricing logic, the process of initiating and making payments for foreign trade transactions were discussed internally and with the bank's customers.

KEY FINDINGS

The analysis of each product's profit growth potential produced a diverse picture. While some products displayed no significant potential for profit increases, others demonstrated a clear opportunity. Figure 8.2 shows a typical price-response and revenue function for a product with clear profit potential from price increases, highlighting the effect of alternative pricing on its profitability.

In this example, if the foreign bank doubled the price from €5 to €10 per transaction, the transaction volume would reduce by 35 percent but the revenue would increase by 50 percent, and profits would increase by more than threefold!

As the products were very labour intensive, the price change had an additional benefit. Less business was being acquired and transacted (but at

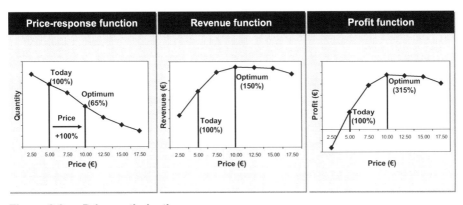

Figure 8.2   Price optimization

a greater profit margin due to the price increase); therefore, the bank could reduce its resources in this area.

The second goal of the project was to ensure that prices reflected the costs occurred. The analysis of the pricing logic used when the original prices were developed clearly showed that the nature of the business and the way in which it was priced were not aligned. Pricing was mostly based on the value of the transaction, following the idea that the bank should be able to charge more for larger deals (i.e. more important to the customer). This principle was, however, quite contrary to the goal of aligning prices with costs.

The subsequent cost analysis showed that the key price drivers were the time required to acquire and complete a trade and the special knowledge required due to the complexity of the transaction. Both are, however, entirely independent of the value of the transaction. A more meaningful driver for pricing is the complexity of the financial instrument being used. Complexity (for example, the number of partners involved in the trade or the number of process steps to be completed) determines not only the time necessary to complete the trade, but also the level of product competency required. By focusing only on the value of a trade, lower-value business was often traded too cheaply and the high-value business too expensively.

The principle of aligning prices with costs was implemented by creating a modular pricing structure. The products were categorized according to their complexity, using a modular product design. In addition to the basic product, more complex products could be crafted by selecting modules. As modules are selected, the overall price increased. This enabled the bank for the first time to link their cost drivers to the customer's actual product usage: each customer was able to decide whether the supplementary product components – security, comfort, etc. – were worth the additional cost.

To ensure that the bank benefits more from large volume deals, a risk management component was included in which the interest rate charged was dependent on the value of the transaction, the credit-worthiness of the customer and other key risk-drivers.

IMPLEMENTATION

These pricing changes went hand in hand with internal staff reductions supplemented by a redesign of internal business processes. In addition, changes were made in the rebate allowance structure, allowing for further price increases. Externally, the structural price changes were communicated using a "signaling" strategy to prepare market participants for the planned price increases.

Value-added checking account packages

BACKGROUND AND GOALS

A regional bank faced the challenge of completely changing the checking accounts it offered. The current product portfolio, consisting of six different accounts, had developed over years of product and market landscape changes. Increasing competitive pressure (from direct and online banks) as well as changing customer behavior ("cherry picking", greater customer willingness-to-switch) meant that a comprehensive analysis of the marketplace was needed. The following issues supported the need for this analysis:

- Drain of significant asset volumes.

- New, attractive, innovative competitive offerings.

- Lack of a specific offering for price-sensitive customers to meet their basic needs.

- High fixed costs and low marginal costs (potential for exploiting economies of scale).

The goal of the analysis was to answer the following questions:

- What strategic goals should management pursue with the new price models?

- How many different price models should be offered in the future?

- Do customers want a specific online-only checking account?

- Which services should be bundled into the various account packages?

- What are the optimal price levels and price intervals between the various accounts (considering segment-specific preferences and customer willingness-to-pay)?

- What is the customer retention rate, that is, how many customers is the bank losing or winning due to the new price models?

- Is the introduction of new checking account packages economically feasible? What is the target profitability with the new prices?

- How can key implementation issues be solved?

APPROACH

These questions were answered by combining the external customer view with the bank's internal expertise. Account managers were brought into the process at an early stage. This allowed both the incorporation of important sales related aspects as well as early motivation of the account managers to support the implementation. For the analysis to integrate an internal and external perspective, expert judgment and customer questionnaires, as well as the utilization of many different data and information sources and methodologies were used. The pricing aspects that were most difficult to quantify (preferences, willingness-to-pay, price elasticity) could thus be analyzed more reliably. The process of optimizing the account prices was carried out in four phases (see Figure 8.3), from strategic goal-setting to management recommendations on how the accounts should be designed.

Based on the various data, information sources, and the results obtained from the analysis, a series of specific recommendations were developed for the future pricing and design of the checking account packages.

KEY FINDINGS

The first step in reconfiguring the checking account packages was to create clarity in the strategic goals. This is essential for any professional price and product design. This requirement may sound trivial, but it often presents significant problems for management teams. For this reason, a workshop with the bank's senior management was held to develop and discuss various strategic goals, and subsequently, to prioritize them based on consensus (see Figure 8.4).

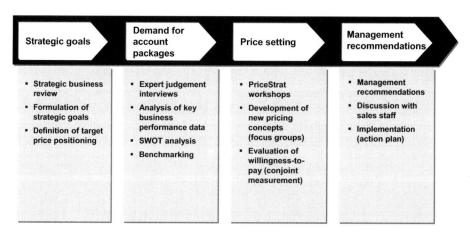

Figure 8.3   Process to analyze and optimize account packages

Strategic goals for new account packages	Participants										
	1	2	3	4	5	6	7	8	9	10	Avg.
1 Customer retention/stronger customer relationships	50	30	22	45	35	50	35	25	30	20	34.2
2 Competitive response/fend of aggressive competitiors	15	0	25	15	5	20	20	15	15	20	15.0
3 Acquisition 'fresh money'/existing customers	5	0	5	10	5	20	10	15	10	10	9.0
4 Acquisition 'fresh money'/new customers	10	25	22	10	0	0	15	5	5	10	10.2
5 Broadening of customer relationship/cross-selling	5	0	2	0	30	0	0	5	5	5	5.2
6 More aggressive (price-)positioning in the market	0	0	0	5	5	0	0	5	0	5	2.0
7 Stronger use of online channel by existing customers	0	0	2	0	0	0	0	5	0	0	0.7
8 Experience with new products	15	45	22	15	20	10	20	25	35	30	23.7

Figure 8.4   Strategic goals for the new account models

The highest priority was assigned to increasing the loyalty of the bank's most attractive customers (34.2 percent). Senior management aimed to use the new account packages to fend off aggressive competitors (23.7 percent) and to gain assets from existing customers (15 percent) and new customers (9 percent) as a secondary priority. An analysis revealed that numerous important customers had switched to competitors and consequently the bank's asset volumes had dropped significantly.

Based on these goals, aided by workshops and focus groups, new concepts were developed and tested using a detailed and comprehensive customer survey (which included a conjoint measurement). The complex questioning technique resulted in reliable customer information (on the willingness-to-switch, willingness-to-pay, price elasticity, importance of online services, preference and utility functions). Based on this information (costs, competitors' products and pricing, etc.), a market simulation model was developed and used to determine the optimal product features and pricing for several account models.

RESULTS

The resulting checking account offering consisted of three models ("basic", "select" and "premium"). The monthly account fees were derived by analyzing customer willingness-to-pay and the associated costs. The bank's profit increased by more than $2 million per year, directly resulting from this project. By reducing the complexity (three models fewer than in the previous product portfolio), employee and customer satisfaction also increased.

An innovative securities price model for private banking (B2B sector)

BACKGROUND AND GOALS

Similar to other sectors, the real net output ratio of institutions in the banking sector has been continually falling. This trend is particularly visible in smaller institutions which, without the benefit of economies of scale, can no longer produce increasingly complex services and rely on external providers instead.

The financial services institution in this case is one of the leading providers in the securities business and offers its products and services to large corporations and other banks. It also offers a range of additional services such as IT solutions, research and training. The existing pricing model was designed in such a way that the income from the core services was used to finance add-on services. This cross-subsidising led to relatively high prices of the core services.

This form of pricing is widespread in the banking sector. For example, in the securities business, financial advisory fees are rarely made explicit; i.e. fees are often integrated into custodian fees or transaction prices. These types of cross-subsidizing business models become threatened when new competitors enter the marketplace and focus on offering only core trading services. Without the add-ons, they are clearly able to offer lower prices. New market entrants normally focus their attention on larger customers, threatening a significant portion of the existing players' core customer base. This was the position that the bank in question found itself in, important customers had already been lost and more customers were being aggressively pursued by new entrants.

Against this background, the following three goals were established for a new price model:

1.   To improve competitiveness by reducing the cross-subsidation. This is done by reducing the costs of the core services and introducing cost-based prices for the additional services.

2.   To increase customer loyalty by rewarding additional volume (following the quid pro quo principle), thus incentivizing growth.

3.   To cross-sell additional services more effectively by using innovative product and price structures (for example, product bundling).

APPROACH

Following a comprehensive review, the concept for a new pricing model, which met the goals set out above, was created. During the first strategic meetings with management, it was decided to retain the pricing per unit principle, which had been used until that point. This meant charging an annual fee for each security position in the customer's portfolio. In the past, attempts to change to a volume-dependent pricing had not been accepted by management as it would have required significant changes in IT systems.

Following this fundamental decision, various alternative price models were developed and critically examined and refined by product management and sales. In the process of assessing these various alternatives, their attractiveness from the customers' perspective, their technical feasibility, and their alignment with strategic goals was considered. By including account management early on in the pricing process, both market and customer knowledge was incorporated, ensuring that the new price model would be well received.

The new price model for the securities business was volume-based. The price a customer was charged depended on the number of transactions traded per year and growth in assets held (see Figure 8.5). This meant that not only large customers, but also rapidly growing smaller customers benefited from lower unit prices. For safe deposits, the pricing structure was changed from

Price per transaction	Annual growth				
	up to 10%	10% to 20%	20% to 30%	30% to 40%	over 40%
up to X	x + 6	x + 5.5	x + 5	x + 4.5	x + 4
X to Y	x + 5	x + 4.5	x + 4	x + 3.5	x + 3
Y to Z	x + 4	x + 3.5	x + 3	x + 2.5	x + 2
Z to T	x + 3	x + 2.5	x + 2	x + 1.5	x + 1
more than T	x + 2	x + 1.5	x + 1	x + 0.5	x

(Number of transactions — row axis label)

Figure 8.5   Basic structure of the new pricing model for securities

a fixed price system to a two part price structure. The aim of this structural change was to make the price increase less transparent (at that point in time, the safe deposit business for the bank did not cover its costs).

After the basic price structure had been set up, the price levels and the rebate levels were established. To meet this need, a "decision support system" with transaction data and price elasticities for important price elements was developed. This system showed the revenue effects of the change from the old to the new price model.

The database used for calculations and optimizations included transaction data for all products in the new price model on an individual customer level for two purchasing periods (required to incorporate the growth dimension of the new price model). For each customer, the volume of transactions across the various securities products, the volume of transactions per channel (online versus in branch) as well as the total dollar value of securities held was captured. This data was then assessed using the current prices in order to produce a breakdown of individual income generated from each customer. The difference between actual income and income estimated from the new price model was minimal; an indication of the high quality of the database. This base scenario was locked into the new price model so that the portfolio data would only be assessed using the new prices. The resulting incomes were calculated on an individual customer level. In this way, management was able to analyze the effects of the new pricing system on revenues and perform a detailed win/loss analysis. By varying the pricing levels and rebate levels, many price scenarios could be assessed.

The process described so far has assumed that price and quantity are independent variables. However, this is quite a naïve assumption, which is why price elasticities and price-volume relationships were integrated into the decision support system. Analysis showed that customers who experienced price reductions under the new pricing system significantly increased their usage, whereas customers with increased prices reduced their usage. Expert judgment estimates were used to identify the relationship between price and quantity (i.e. the price elasticity). A representative sample of customers was selected and the respective account managers estimated their reaction to each adjustment in price. This estimation was done for the most important products. The information was then aggregated and entered into the decision-support model.

KEY FINDINGS

A general problem in switching from an old to a new pricing system is that it always leads to "winners and losers". The institution wanted to achieve an income-neutral change and wanted to minimize the number of both "winners" and "losers". The price levels and rebate levels of the new price model were set accordingly. In total, around 7 percent of existing customers were "losers", and around 3 percent of existing customers were better off than before ("winners"). The average price per transaction dropped by around 25 percent in order to re-establish competitiveness. Management increased the price of their custodian services by around 10 percent, ensuring for the first time that costs were covered.

The prices for some additional services were also increased significantly. To the customers, the fee change remained intransparent, since certain services were offered only as part of a package. In determining prices for these additional services, cost, customer willingness-to-pay, and the strategic importance of the services were taken into account. Overall, the time required from the beginning of the project to final sign off by senior management was around five months.

IMPLEMENTATION

An important aspect of the implementation of the new price model was the question of how the discounts of the new price systems would be granted. Since the unit price in the new model was dependent on the number of transactions and the annual growth of transactions, it was important to clarify whether each customer should pay a price corresponding to his previous year's performance, or whether each customer should first pay the highest price and then receive a refund at the end of the year. Management opted for the refund model due to its ease of implementation. In addition, this model was used to strengthen the customer relationship by giving the customer the choice to receive a refund in cash or to use the money to buy additional services valued at twice the amount of the refund.

Secondly, the technical feasibility of the new price model had to be guaranteed, and a professional internal and external communication program had to be developed. Therefore, a specifications sheet for the technical implementation was generated, and the required reprogramming of the trading system was performed. For the external communication, the marketing department produced a comprehensive brochure in which the services and the new price system were described in detail. To introduce the new price model, the account managers were professionally trained. Additionally, support materials including suggested selling arguments and a set of "Frequently Asked Questions" were developed. With the help of a migration model, the account managers could communicate the effects of the changes to their customers. To this end, planning workshops were held with selected customers to strengthen the relationship and to show ways to manage prices at a moderate level. These activities enabled the new scheme to be well accepted by customers and led to greater customer satisfaction. Income stabilized and many lost customers were won back.

New securities price model in brokerage

BACKGROUND AND GOALS

When two banks undergo a merger, they are faced with the challenge of integrating teams, business processes and product portfolios. In this case study, two banks, one focused on retail banking services and the other bank on private banking, merged. Interestingly, the product and customer portfolios of the two banks significantly overlapped each other. While products were steadily blended together in the first few years following the merger, existing customers holding the products continued to be charged according to each banks' price models. This presented the following three problems:

- Uncertainty for sales reps about which price model was appropriate for a given customer.

- Lack of transparency of the services included in the different securities models.

- Management problems in controlling disparate sales forces as the incentives for customer advisors differed according to each pricing model.

Thus, the aim of the project was to develop a clear and unified price model. It was important that the shift from the old to the new price models would not significantly impact revenue or the number of customer "winners" and "losers". Customer and advisor satisfaction should be increased and customer retention should be improved.

APPROACH

The project had two phases. During the first phase, the key components of the new pricing model were developed. The second phase focused on optimizing the various price points. Interviews and workshops with product management and sales were held in phase 1 to help arrive at a new price model. The results were then discussed with senior management. During the workshops, the strengths and weaknesses of the existing price models were identified and a set of pricing guidelines which would act as a framework for the new price model were developed. One of these pricing guidelines stated that the new price model should be introduced with minimum "noise", implying that the new model should incorporate as many elements of the present models as possible (especially those which were considered strengths). The basic structure of the new model was constructed from the results from these workshops and was discussed and refined with all stakeholders involved.

In phase 2, the concrete price levels, for example, minimum fees, provisions and discount limits, were set. Key information for this task came from a comprehensive benchmarking study, customer questionnaire, and individual customer deposit and transaction data.

The benchmarking study examined the actual and target positioning of the bank within the competitive environment, considering pricing for individual products as well as across the entire customer relationship. To account for overall customer relationships, individual price structures and levels were compared and sample customer calculations and a segment analysis were made. The segment analysis was particularly valuable because it took into account different price components that only applied when certain asset and transaction thresholds were reached. Figure 8.6 is an example of a comparison of online brokerage competitors (differentiated according to customer segment). This type of benchmarking helps identify the potential for price increases.

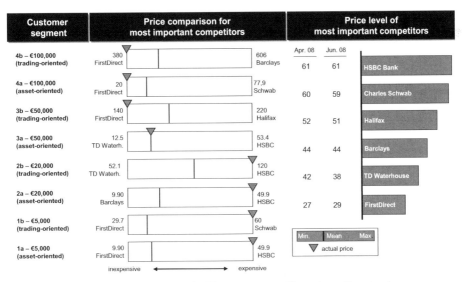

Figure 8.6   Price comparison of different competitors in online brokerage

The aim of the customer questionnaire was to determine customers' price sensitivity to individual price components and to test how different price models would impact sales decisions and overall attractiveness. In total, 1,200 actual and potential customers from all segments completed the questionnaire in face-to-face interviews. Multivariate methodologies such as Conjoint Measurement were used alongside standard market research methods. In this way, management obtained valid statements about price elasticity, willingness-to-switch as well as other important value drivers. Subsequently, product management created a database with individual customer data, containing information on all deposits and transactions. This database on a customer level was then used to analyze the effect of the new price model on income (based on the current model) and likely customer migration. Based on the transaction data, the database calculated what each customer's fee was with the original pricing model. The customers were then "migrated" to the new price model and the price was updated. This procedure enabled management to categorize each customer as a "winner" or a "loser" of the new model, and the total income for the new price system was calculated. Integrating the information on price elasticity from the questionnaire, the rate of growth (or loss) in the customers over different price levels could be realistically simulated. Using the database, multiple scenarios were simulated and presented to senior management for discussion and final decision.

KEY RESULTS

The new price model consisted of three individual charges (see Figure 8.7). Choice A had a low price for deposits (basic fee) and a high price per transaction (no change from the old model), whereas Choice C had a high price for deposits and transactions were free (100 percent rebate). Customers were now able to select the pricing structure which was most in line with their expected usage. Customers who traded less were recommended to opt for Choice A. Choice C was designed for "heavy traders". Customers were able to switch their preferred pricing structure quarterly.

As shown in Figure 8.7, the three pricing structures differ in the level of each price component. Management also considered differentiating price structures based on the services provided (for example, consultancy, support, information provided or reporting). However, it proved difficult to identify valuable services for the retail segment which would have allowed the bank to differentiate the choices. Among those services, consultancy services were considered the only option for differentiation. Based on the results from the customer questionnaire, management decided not to include a separate "consultancy" price component, but to include it in the basic fee instead.

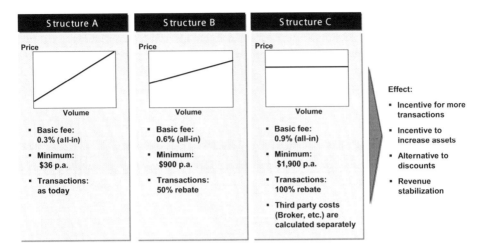

Figure 8.7   Basic structure of the new securities price model

The price levels were chosen in such a way that there was always a competitively priced structure for each customer usage pattern (combination of volume of deposits and number of transactions). In addition, the various pricing tiers were simplified. For example, for custodian services, certain types of securities were bundled together and no longer priced individually. As a result of the new price model, income increased by 5 percent, with around 10 percent of customers as "losers" and 5 percent "winners".

IMPLEMENTATION

A number of departments within the bank were involved in implementing the price model simultaneously. This included marketing, legal, HR, finance, the call center as well as other key areas (IT, key account management and product management). Questions that were raised in this phase were resolved by the project team or within the specific departments. This can be illustrated by two examples:

1.   Hard versus soft migration: in general, there are two ways to migrate customers from old to new pricing models. A "hard" migration moves all customers to the new price model immediately, whereas a "soft" migration offers customers the option to change to the new price model or remain in the old one. For new customers, though, only the new model would apply. The advantages and disadvantages of each option were analyzed and discussed thoroughly with the departments involved. In this case, management opted for a soft migration because IT did not have the capacity to pull off a hard migration in the short term. Furthermore, the risk of alienating customers and sales was considered to be too high.

2.   Business Training: the bank could no longer train its entire sales force directly from headquarters. A waterfall approach was chosen instead. A select few experienced employees were given comprehensive training from the headquarters and then given the responsibility to train group leaders in the field ("train the trainers" concept).

The entire pricing process took around a year (from initial ideas to implementation). The implementation of the model ran smoothly and feedback from account managers and customers was very positive. The quality of the project and its approach was confirmed six months after its introduction: around 50 percent of existing customers had migrated to the new model, either on the advice of their account managers or by their own choice.

Intelligent price and growth model in private banking

BACKGROUND AND GOALS

The price structures for securities transactions in a private bank had developed over 10 years prior and no longer met customer requirements. The demands of the bank's customers had undergone significant changes over the years as a result of an increased level in market transparency and accessible information. Previously, investors could frequently only obtain recommendations from their own bank, whereas nowadays they have access to countless channels of information, allowing customer segments with unique needs to develop over time (for example, "self-directed" customers with information needs or with personal advice needs). Traditionally, the bank securities business had charged brokerage fees as a percentage of the total transaction volume. With that fee, the bank covered both transaction and customer advisory services costs.

However, the bank's heavy traders, who did not have the need for the advisory service, were no longer willing to pay these (relatively) high fees. In order to keep customers, sales granted extensive discounts which could not be explained by objective parameters, such as capital invested. Some competitors introduced price models that combined an annual fee (in some cases bundled with the deposit fee) with a relatively low transaction fee. Our client could no longer evade this trend and decided to implement a similar new pricing model. Management pursued several goals with the new model:

- To review the existing price models.

- To design and evaluate alternatives.

- To optimize price levels and price structures using internal data and customer questionnaires.

- To develop recommendations for developing new price models in the securities business.

- To conceptualize implementation measures.

APPROACH

During the review of the existing flat fee model, product managers and account managers collaborated to identify the following drawbacks:

- Limitation of number of transactions: the number of transactions included in the flat fee model was capped at too low a level, reducing the attractiveness of the service for the actual target group, the heavy traders.

- Too many services included: in addition to the securities transactions, the flat-fee also covered many other banking transactions which customers focused on trading regard as superfluous.

- Too expensive: the price levels were too high so that sales were only made possible by granting considerable discounts.

In a next step, new concepts were developed to resolve the weaknesses identified. To ensure the consistency of the project with the overall business strategy, general principles for the structure and desired effects of the new price model were set in a senior management workshop. The most important pricing principles included:

- Every customer should be able to choose a pricing model which corresponds to his specific needs ("self-selection").

- Price structures should be transparent, but should not be directly comparable to the competition.

- Each customer relationship should be profitable (in contrast to: each product should be profitable).

- In order to stabilize revenues, future pricing systems should contain more fixed instead of variable price components (example: fixed asset-based fees instead of transaction dependent fees).

Based on these principles, new price concepts were developed in several product management workshops where both the breadth of services to be included in each package (i.e. types of securities) and the level of price reduction for securities were discussed. The resulting concepts allowed the customer to choose between various options with fixed and variable prices (non-linear pricing).

The concepts shown in Figure 8.8 for four different customer segments made it possible to optimally skim customer willingness-to-pay. Freedom to choose meant that every customer can select the model best suited to his or her needs and that he or she was not forced into a suboptimal price model, e.g. based on asset volume. The previous flat fee for the bank's other services was unbundled from the securities transaction fees (a separate concept was developed for this). With the modular structure of services, the problem of customers paying for unwanted services was solved, and at the same time the concept of "self-selection" was supported. The annual limit on the number of transactions was waived and replaced by a price model in which third-party costs were billed separately. This made it possible to effectively hedge against risk costs without creating a negative effect for heavy traders trying to abuse the system. It should be noted that the IT expenditures in this case were low. Usually, price systems in which the costs vary considerably with actual usage are expensive to implement and to maintain.

A customer questionnaire was subsequently administered to further refine the concepts and to detect the optimal pricing levels. In order to model real customer behaviour, a sales process was simulated in the questionnaire. In the first phase, the concepts were presented on a computer screen without any price information and customers were asked about the attractiveness of the individual product offerings. The "Silver 50" concept failed this test and was thus discontinued. In the next step, the van Westendorp methodology was

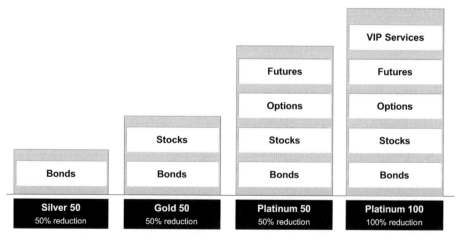

Figure 8.8   Private banking packages

used to determine customer willingness-to-pay. Thirdly, customer willingness-to-purchase was evaluated by presenting three price scenarios (high, medium and low price level) to the respondents. The differences between the prices of each model were kept constant for all three scenarios. Optimal prices were determined by using an elasticity analysis (see Figure 8.9).

When the price was changed from a high to a medium price level, customer demand was elastic enough in order to compensate for lower prices, resulting in a higher profit. In contrast, the elasticity for the second price change, from medium to low, was not high enough to generate any additional profit.

The optimal price distances between models were established by comparing the preferences ascertained from the first question on attractiveness with actual willingness-to-pay. (Example: if a price model was chosen proportionally less often in all three scenarios compared to the price-independent preferences, then the price gap had to be lowered for the other models.) To validate these price levels, the results were compared to the van Westendorp analysis, which confirmed the findings.

To assess the impact of introducing the new price models, the findings of the customer questionnaire were linked to the actual (in this case previous year) usage. One possible caveat in allowing customers to choose their pricing option is that customers only select a model if the total costs are lower than before. However, the analysis clearly demonstrated that numerous customers

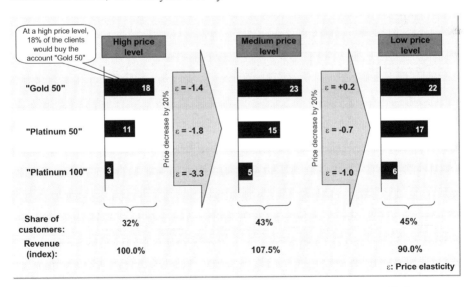

Figure 8.9   Optimization of the new concept's price and product offering

were willing to pay more money if they were offered more value by the new offering. Overall, the analysis indicated that introducing the new price models would increase income from the securities business by 10–15 percent.

KEY RESULTS

The new price models brought about the following improvements for the bank's securities business:

- Higher leverage of customer willingness-to-pay by introducing segment-specific offers and the freedom of choice.

- Incentives to increase usage by lowering variable costs.

- Hedging against risk by settling third-party costs separately.

- Optimal price levels based on elasticity analysis.

- Increase in income from securities business by more than 10 percent.

- Profit stabilization through a higher share of fixed price components.

In addition, customer satisfaction was increased due to the following benefits:

- Models based on customer needs.

- Cost control through fixed costs (the flat-fee).

- Transparency and simplicity.

- Freedom of choice.

- Lower prices for higher usage (economies of scale).

IMPLEMENTATION

As the new price models were based on the principle of freedom of choice, there was no need to apply pressure on customers to migrate, save the existing flat-fee customers. The flat-fee customers were offered the new "Platinum 100" model for their securities business plus the (modular) flat-fee for their other banking services. For rest of the customers, a migration plan (see Figure 8.10) was created based on their usage profile. Their advisors could access a migration tool to recommend an optimal model, however, "optimal" in this case does not necessarily mean the model with the lowest costs for the customers (this type of migration is rarely profitable for a bank). Hence, the migration tool was

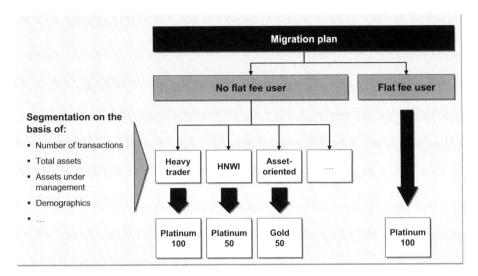

Figure 8.10   Migration plan

built to give a recommendation which provides the customer with the highest incentives (based on their actual usage) to increase their trading in securities and/or to transfer assets from another bank.

Additional components of the new model's implementation were a detailed communication plan (channels, contents, time plan) and the training of account managers, something particularly important for private banking institutions since the relationship between customers and their advisors is often the most important factor in buying decisions (buying decisions heavily based on the advisors' recommendations).

The new pricing models were implemented just nine months after the start of the project and were well received by customers.

CONCLUSION

Many banks shy away from giving customers the freedom to choose their own price model because they are afraid of losing profit if the customers choose the least costly model. This case study shows, however, that by detailed analysis of actual usage and expected customer behavior (using internal data and customer questionnaires) together with carefully planned implementation, this risk can be minimized. On the contrary, with the outlined measures, banks can reduce price pressure on securities business and realize consistent and stable increases in revenues through intelligent customer incentives.

Price transparency and monitoring in retail banking

BACKGROUND AND GOALS

Mortgage pricing at this credit facility was heavily oriented towards costs and less towards customer willingness-to-pay. In particular, the management team had little foundation for making qualified pricing decisions – there was no transparency on current pricing practices. Senior managers could only accurately determine how many customers were granted discounts on their mortgages rates or how large the discounts were through significant manual effort. Since the accessibility of suitable data was low, pricing decisions were deferred or not made at all.

Knowing this, the management team had two aims:

1.   To create transparency on the number and level of discounts and rebates granted.

2.   To develop a monitoring tool to guarantee future transparency, support price decisions, and control overzealous discount granting by the sales force.

APPROACH

The project had three phases: first, the information needed to conduct the analysis was defined in detailed interviews with IT and finance managers. The company kept considerable data, but it was located in various departments and systems (P&L, MIS, CRM), so it was consolidated into a pricing database after validation. In the second phase, interviews and workshops were held with the key stakeholders to discuss the importance and validity of the data. Thirdly, the data was analyzed and a set of tools was developed to monitor discounts.

KEY RESULTS

The most important results for the credit facility were:

*   Improved transparency on the level and structure of discounts and rebates on mortgage loans.

*   An integrated pricing database enabling future analysis.

*   Clear rules for account managers for offering discounts and rebates in the future.

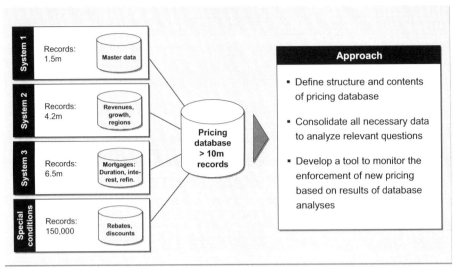

Figure 8.11   Pricing database

- A monitoring instrument for supporting account managers.

- An increase in profit of over 2 percent in the mortgage business.

Account manager satisfaction was also increased as a result of the following benefits and newly added IT applications:

- Price-sensitivity tool to better understand the effects of interest rate changes on profit.

- Calculation tool to illustrate the customer net present value.

- Clear incentive structure oriented to corporate profitability.

- Early involvement of account managers in developing these applications.

IMPLEMENTATION

The advisors used the price sensitivity tool in preparation for meetings with customers to calculate the potential effects of a drop in interest rates on profit. This improved source of information was an important tool in negotiating interest rates with customers. Clear rules on granting rebates and discounts allowed the necessary flexibility during negotiations. The tool demonstrated the revenue contribution, products uptake, and the level of rebates or discounts being given on a customer level, enabling the bank to improve its customer orientation and increase the satisfaction of the sales team.

Brand premium in corporate banking

BACKGROUND AND GOALS

A financial institution's brand serves as a clear differentiator to its competitors. As in many other areas, financial services are becoming more and more commoditized to the point that it has become almost impossible to tell the difference between checking accounts, and credit cards are offering almost identical APRs and rewards programs. Against this background, "the value-add" of financial institutions' brands are becoming more important. The following case study focuses on determining and quantifying the value-add of a strong brand. We analyzed the following questions for a large corporate banking customer:

- What drives the value-add of the bank's brand?

- Based on the brand value-add, what price premiums can be charged for selected services?

- Are there any differences in the brand value drivers between individual customer segments, and how can these segments be identified?

- How is the value-add of the brand realized, i.e. what measures can be taken to achieve a higher price premium to better extract the brand's value?

APPROACH

The "brand value-add" or "brand premium" measures customers' additional willingness-to-pay for a bank's product or service compared to its competitors. In other words, the brand premium describes the price difference that can be realized directly resulting from the value of a bank's brand. Figure 8.12 shows a typical process for measuring the brand premium for selected commercial banking products.

The main stage in determining the brand premium involves obtaining information on customers' willingness-to-pay and on brand value drivers in a customer questionnaire. In this specific case, over 200 corporate customers were interviewed, using conjoint measurement. Customers and non-customers were presented with "trade-offs" of different product scenarios, where the brand, price, and range of services differed. The respondents were provided with increasingly complex trade-offs based on their responses (for more information on conjoint measurement, see Chapter 4). The challenge when using this

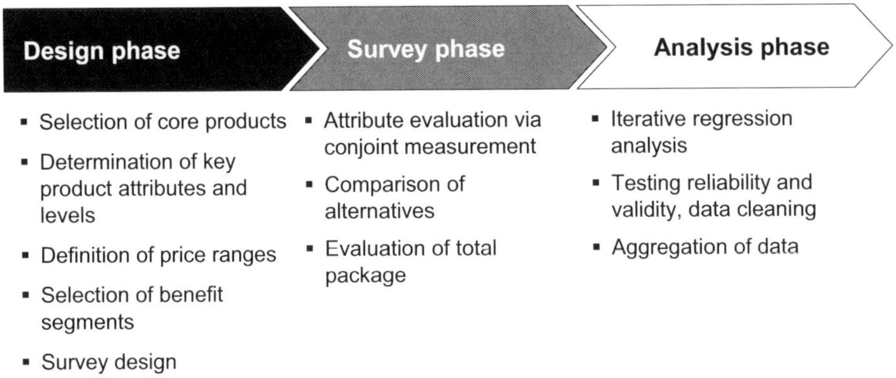

Design phase	Survey phase	Analysis phase
• Selection of core products	• Attribute evaluation via conjoint measurement	• Iterative regression analysis
• Determination of key product attributes and levels	• Comparison of alternatives	• Testing reliability and validity, data cleaning
• Definition of price ranges	• Evaluation of total package	• Aggregation of data
• Selection of benefit segments		
• Survey design		

Figure 8.12 Process for measuring the brand premium

particular method to determine the brand premium is to choose the right core products to analyze and to choose the appropriate price levels for each product and customer segment. In preliminary conversations with internal experts in the bank, several products were selected using various criteria, including: revenue contribution, customer needs and potential for profit improvements. These products were then evaluated and prioritized in workshops with the sales team.

KEY RESULTS

Sample results of this type of analysis – quantified brand premiums for specific products over similar products of its main competitors – are shown in Figure 8.13. In this case, a brand premium of up to 50 basis points was calculated for the bank's business loans. This value differs, as expected, for different customer segments and competitors (for example, principal customers of the bank, secondary customers, and non-customers assign different brand premiums to the bank in comparison to competitor A).

The results of the conjoint analysis were aggregated in a distribution function and analyzed further in a simulation model. Based on the simulations, optimal price increments were derived for various products (high-end versus low-priced product alternatives) or for different segments, defined by descriptive variables such as credit-worthiness, region or length of business relationship.

Almost more important than determining optimal price levels was the knowledge gained about the drivers of brand premium (the "brand value drivers"), such as the quality of advice or the extent of customer orientation. First, potential key factors were collected based on various sources of information (benchmarking, analysis of customer satisfaction). These were

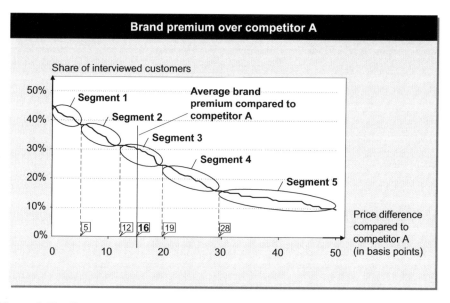

Figure 8.13   Segment-specific brand premium

then further discussed and prioritized with the sales staff from various regions during workshops. Early input from the bank's sales teams was important so that the customer perspective was taken into account from early stages. This also helped ensure a seamless implementation of the price changes. The result from these workshops was a list of more than twenty potential value drivers which were then further evaluated in customer interviews. As many of the interviewees held business relationships with more than one bank, it was possible to directly compare the performance of several banks on the brand value drivers.

IMPLEMENTATION

The results of the analyses were implemented in close cooperation with sales and marketing. On top of adjusting the price levels based on the results of the conjoint study, the knowledge gained on brand value drivers was used to improve the price and value implementation, i.e. supporting the sales force in performing better in price negotiations with customers. An action plan was developed to identify each customer segment's willingness-to-pay and relevant brand value drivers during the negotiation. For that purpose, with input from the sales representatives, a series of sales guidelines highlighting the value drivers were developed and translated into arguments to be used in sales negotiations. In addition, a joint workshop with sales yielded several tools to support the communication of brand value drivers in conversations with customers.

CONCLUSION

Many companies in the financial services sector lack a tool to measure their brand value and brand premium. As many financial products and services are becoming increasingly commoditized, this information is crucial for optimal price setting decisions and improved price implementation. By using sophisticated research methods like conjoint analysis, the value of a brand and the drivers of this value can be precisely measured.

Smart pricing for investment funds

BACKGROUND AND GOALS

Over the last few years, competition in the investment funds market has been steadily increasing. More and more, foreign competition has flooded into domestic markets and threatened established players with aggressive prices and aggressive sales commissions. On top of this, performance metrics and other market data is becoming more transparent than ever to investors. Competitive products give customers new alternatives, promising returns that incumbent funds can not match. In light of these difficult market conditions, many incumbent providers have attempted to reduce costs in order to lower their cost-income ratio. To date, many have made substantial progress focusing on process and structural changes.

However, most have now exhausted their ability to cut costs any further. Going forward, the need for more to be done on the revenue side both in terms of volume and pricing is universally recognized. This case study outlines the potential that can be effectively realized by pragmatic price optimization and by introducing new sales commission structures.

APPROACH

The key to price optimization is determining price elasticities of the various customer segments and understanding the dynamics of price changes in different investment fund categories. Changing the management fee of a fixed income bond fund by one percent, for example, will have a greater impact on volume than the same one percent change in management fee of an equity fund. In this case study, the necessary price elasticity data was determined using pragmatic tools such as the SKP revenue-risk matrix and expert judgment (SKP PriceStrat).

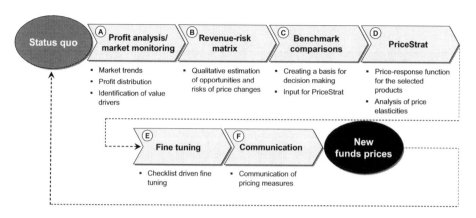

Figure 8.14   Process for optimizing fund pricing

Using internal market and profit monitoring data and the revenue-risk matrix, a cross-divisional team from finance, product management, and sales selected a number of relevant funds for further analysis. These selections were based on the revenue potential from price changes (resulting from the funds overall size) as well as the need for re-pricing (e.g. due to aggressive competitive offers). Within the context of an expert judgment workshop, the funds' price elasticities were analyzed using the PriceStrat methodology. The output of such an exercise is an initial internal price elasticity estimate for each fund (see Figure 8.15 for an example of the results from a PriceStrat exercise).

The next step was the methodological challenge of optimizing the management fee of the investment funds, i.e. analyzing the so-called "price-performance effect". Unlike many other financial products, a fund's perceived quality (i.e. its performance) is not independent of its management fee. For example, the "perceived quality" of a checking account, a credit card, or even a mortgage product is not a function of its price. In fund management, on the other hand, an increase in the management fee automatically reduces the funds relative performance, thus this effect must be taken into account when optimizing investment fund fees.

Consequently, since performance and competitive ranking of the fund will impact its perceived quality (i.e. performance), and thus the price elasticity of a fund, optimizing prices for investment funds is especially difficult. Hence, internal experts from performance measurement (asset management) and product management teams had to carefully consider the consequences of price changes on various parameters.

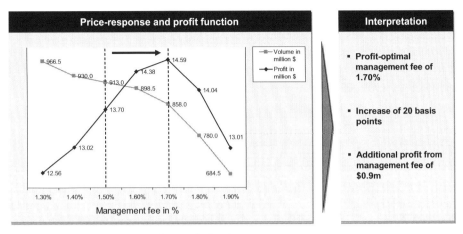

Figure 8.15 Management fee optimization

KEY RESULTS

Using this approach, management fees for over one hundred core products of the fund company were analyzed and optimized. In many instances, the PriceStrat results indicated significant potential for price increases. In other instances, a reduction in management fees was optimal. The subsequent analysis of the "price-performance effect" indicated that many of the price changes would not create a significant change in fund performance or its competitive ranking. In most cases, market-based fluctuations in the price of the fund itself would influence the fund's performance or its competitive ranking far more than any changes to the management fee could do. In all, a total profit potential in the tens of millions of dollars was identified.

IMPLEMENTATION

The key to implementing these fee changes in the marketplace was to work closely with the sales and marketing teams. The trick was to communicate the price changes intelligently to distribution partners by integrating the fee changes within a redesign of the sales commission system. The goal of the new sales commission system was to create a clearer level of differentiation in terms of profit contribution at both a product and sales channel partner level. In the past, competitive pressures had led some of the company's most important distribution partners ("A-partners") to completely or partially shift sales and assets to competitors. A revamped sales commission system was considered critical to retain or win back these A-partners. With the help of a simulation model, different commission systems and individual commission levels were analyzed. The optimal model was selected jointly with sales, and a comprehensive communication plan was developed to support the communication of the new commission system to the distribution partners. Critical to the success of the new system was to quantify the effects of price changes for each distribution partner (aided by the simulation tool) and clarify important aspects of the price changes in a frequently asked questions document.

CONCLUSION

In the coming years, professional pricing will play a much greater role in the management agendas of fund companies across the world. From a sales perspective, it will become increasingly critical to put the right commission structures into play. Many fund management companies still use a "scatter gun approach" today. In the future, however, it will become necessary to differentiate commission structures by profit contribution, as well as by product or sales channel partner. Prices will then need to be calibrated to cover any incremental commission paid out. In general, fund management companies will need to increase their pricing professionalism by integrating the processes and methods described above. With institutionalized pricing processes, cross-functional teams from fund management, marketing and sales need to constructively work together.

Cost and needs-based packaged solutions in basic banking services

BACKGROUND AND GOALS

The bank in this case study had high costs associated with its basic retail services (checking account, payment transactions, ATM withdrawals, credit and debit cards), and the prices charged to consumers for these services did not cover the cost of service delivery (mailing costs, manual transaction processing costs, ATM network and other IT costs, etc). There was, at least in part, an explanation for this: in return for fee free or inexpensive basic banking services, customers had historically accepted a lower rate of interest on their savings deposits. When the prevailing interest rates were high, net interest income was sufficient to subsidize these basic services, but this changed in a lower interest rate environment. In times when low rates prevailed, the bank found it progressively harder to make money from basic services like checking accounts. Customers that did not adopt the bank's other services (such as securities accounts or mortgages) became unprofitable.

In order to improve the profitability of its checking account business, the bank gradually introduced a series of price increases over a period of a few years. This triggered a negative customer reaction and led to deteriorating levels of customer satisfaction, intensified by strong criticism by press and consumer groups. Thus, the bank went in search of other ways to grow profits.

An initial assessment of the situation suggested that considerable opportunities to reduce costs existed. For example, incentives could be developed to stimulate usage of the bank's online service – a low cost alternative channel providing customers with basic banking services.

The bank wanted to explore if and how differentiated account service levels ("packaged account solutions") could be created and, when priced intelligently, could successfully act as an incentive for customers to switch to low cost solutions and improve customer satisfaction at the same time.

The project goals were specified as follows:

- Develop needs-based "package account solutions" for basic banking services.

- Determine a proper way to allocate different types of costs by product.

- Assess customer acceptance of the solutions.

- Optimize prices for each account package, so that every package is profitable.

APPROACH AND KEY RESULTS

In conjunction with product management teams, products and services from account management, payment transactions, cash transactions, credit and debit cards were selected for inclusion in the analysis. The selection process ensured that products that drove customer value (i.e. debit and credit cards) as well as the banks more cost intensive services (i.e. counter services) would be included in the analysis. A series of workshops with product and account management teams were held in which different account package solutions were discussed, developed and refined.

Secondly, a detailed analysis of costs was carried out to calculate the profitability of the different package options. This was an important step in determining the optimal price structure and price levels. Relative to fixed costs, banks variable costs are generally low. However, from a price structure optimization perspective, variable cost components are important and must be considered. Indeed, the central question in this case was whether to treat the various cost components as variable or fixed. For example, since allocated IT costs were not dependent on actual usage, they were assumed to be fixed costs. Personnel costs, on the other hand, could be viewed as usage dependent (e.g. manual payment processing and teller service staff). As a result, only incremental external transaction costs were considered in determining the cost for online transactions, whereas personnel costs were also taken into account for all over-the-counter transactions.

Once the cost analysis was complete, account package uptake and utilization rates were modelled. Different price level scenarios were analyzed to determine their profit impact. Since no actual customer uptake data was available, assumptions based on rational consumer behavior were made (i.e. based on their needs, customers would choose the most cost effective package). The resulting recommendations for the future account packages are shown in Figure 8.16

The "basic" package developed enabled customers to obtain all basic checking account services (i.e. the package included unlimited transactions, free check safekeeping as well as an ATM card for fee free withdrawals on the bank's network) for a very attractive fee. For all other services, such as a VISA credit card or overdraft protection, customers would have to pay relatively higher prices. To give customers an incentive to increase their online account

Figure 8.16   Implemented account packages

usage (the bank had a high proportion of inactive online accounts), the package included a set of Internet security tools and instruments for transaction analysis that could be accessed online. More demanding customers, for example those who make frequent overseas payments and want a credit card, could opt for upgraded "Silver" or "Gold" packages.

Given the homogeneity of the bank's customer base in terms of usage levels, through careful optimization of price levels, it was determined that the "basic" package could be offered at a relatively low price of $1.99 per month with relatively low risk of revenue or profit losses. The prices of the other packages were set at $4.99 and $9.99 per month, respectively.

As a final step, customer focus groups were held to test overall customer acceptance of the new packages. Customers appreciated the new packages, specifically the opportunity to select from a clear set of needs-orientated packages, lower prices due to the ability to purchase a package based on only the services they need, and improved transparency (this lead to a more positive price image for the bank).

IMPLEMENTATION AND BENEFITS

In contrast to other service providers such as utility providers (telecoms, cable companies, etc.), it is harder for banks to charge a monthly subscription based fee, but they can draw on psychological price effects by communicating prices on a monthly basis. Hence, the bank decided to market prices monthly.

The new package accounts offered the retail bank the following benefits:

- Creation of an incentive for customers to behave in a cost optimal manner.

- Higher levels of customer satisfaction.

- Orientation towards customer needs.

- Product transparency, clarity and simplicity.

- Freedom of choice for customers.

- Better overview of internal cost.

- Positive impact on the banks price image.

- No losses in profit.

Defining master pricing processes in retail and private banking (supported by a pricing process monitoring tool)

BACKGROUND AND GOALS

Professional price management is a key lever of profitability. In addition to developing a deep understanding of pricing topics (for example, price strategy, price optimization methodology, means of price differentiation), a key success factor for achieving pricing excellence is the ability to master the pricing process – the activities and procedures required to make optimal pricing decisions.

In this case study, a successful bank with a focus on retail and private banking aimed to enhance the speed, accuracy and quality of its pricing processes. Pricing decisions were not systematically optimized, and each department in the bank abided to its own (more or less) structured approach. Pricing analyses and price setting were carried out exclusively by the product management team, but no systematic and standardized pricing process existed, nor did a systematic consultation process with other functional units (sales for example). Important pricing information (for example, price elasticities, information about competitors, profitability) had not been collected in a systematic way and consequently was not exploited in the bank's pricing process, and neither guidelines nor rules for implementing prices and controlling price setting existed.

To summarize, the goals of the project were to design and implement a master pricing process and to ensure every step was monitored thoroughly:

1.   Define a master pricing process which encompasses all relevant steps: developing an overall pricing strategy and a strategy for each pricing activity, and establishing techniques for price setting (structure design and level determination), price implementation, and price controlling.

2.   Create an easy to use tool that incorporates each step in the master pricing process. The tool allows pricing managers to steer and monitor the pricing process.

APPROACH

In a first step, Simon-Kucher & Partners, in conjunction with senior management representatives, set the objectives for the future master pricing process as follows:

- To have a common understanding of the required steps in the pricing process and depth of analysis required by clarifying the differences between "tactical" and "strategic" pricing measures, and to clarify which process steps are the responsibility of which organisational units – product management, sales managers, and/or supporting units.

- To clarify which organizational units are involved in the pricing process: who participates in each step? How should the involved parties interact and what role should each play? At what step in the process are they involved (timing)?

- To improve the ability to plan and schedule, leading to faster decisions (avoid process-loops by ensuring that all relevant inputs are available when needed).

- To make processes more reliable by documenting procedures and controlling milestones.

- To make higher quality decisions based on a structured approach, extensive analyses and intensive participation of all relevant specialists.

- To minimize risk for the customer, as well as for the entire bank.

Based on these guidelines, the project team analyzed the current pricing strategy, price setting, implementation, monitoring, and controlling procedures ("status quo analysis") in workshops with key process participants. Through "process mapping", a structured process analysis methodology, all key players were brought together to discuss the current process steps, investigate current problems, and develop possible improvements. These initial ideas served as a blueprint for creating the master pricing process. The main tasks in this step were the definition of key elements in each process (required input, distribution of responsibilities, necessary interfaces, etc.) as well as of process milestones (to be able to control the process and achieve long term sustainability). The differentiation between "tactical" and "strategic" pricing measures was made based on revenue potential and risk of making a poor pricing decision, which were evaluated based on the results of competitive analysis and the market research.

KEY RESULTS AND IMPLEMENTATION

The analysis of several current pricing processes resulted in the development of one common master pricing process for all future pricing measures.

One of the key steps within the master process is the competitive analysis. In this step, all pricing-relevant information about the competition must be gathered, analyzed and made accessible for the pricing decision. The master process also includes recommendations for how to use different analysis tools and how to interpret their results:

- Benchmark on displayed (list) prices: competitors' prices and price structures are compared by calculating prices for a selected set of representative customers with typical usage patterns. If, for example, the analysis shows that certain of the bank's price levels are below average, selective price increases may be warranted, depending on the price elasticity of the product.

- Mystery shopping to uncover enforced prices: in this step, the results of the list price benchmark are augmented by the analysis of real market prices. If the bank's enforced price is below competitors' prices, price enforcement must be analyzed and measures to improve it must be sought.

- Analysis of competitive advantages: customer requirements and the bank's perceived performance relative to the competition must be analyzed. These elements can be visualized in a matrix of competitive advantage to check whether the bank's price positioning is consistent with its performance positioning. Inconsistent positions can be identified, and prices and product/service offers can be adjusted to correct inconsistencies.

A second key step in the process is market research, the collection and analysis of information on the customer. Relevant steps in this phase include:

- Workshops with sales representatives: using the knowledge and experience of the sales department is a simple and fast way to get an initial feeling on how customers would react to price changes. Workshops can be used, for example, to determine price elasticities for different segments or to discuss a new price model.

- Interviews of the sales department can help systematize and quantify the sales team's knowledge.

- Qualitative customer interviews and focus groups are well suited for answering non-quantifiable questions, for example, the perception of a price.

- Third-person customer interviews like the van Westendorp method and conjoint measurement analyses can quantify utility values of certain product attributes and identify price elasticity, customers' willingness-to-pay, and optimal price levels.

The depth of both the competitive and market research analyses depends, among other things, on the expected revenue/profit, the expected risk, and the intensity and complexity of the competition.

After the master process was defined, a pricing process monitoring tool that contained every single step of the pricing process was designed. The tool allows for short cuts between the steps, documents process milestones, and contains checklists and templates to be used for the analysis, business case calculations, and documentation of market research results:

- Decision section: describes the relevance of the pricing measure (strategic or tactical, with explanatory statements), portrays target groups and markets, estimates volume and risk of the pricing measure.

- Benchmarking section: contains a description of the benchmarking process (top five national as well as international competitors), list prices, the bank's price-performance ratio relative to the competitive environment, and a determination of the pricing range the market allows.

- Price-response function section: contains a tool to derive elasticities based on sales team and customer input.

- Business case section: based on all input data (number of existing and new customers, prices, price elasticities and resulting volume effects, real costs, and opportunity costs) a business case calculates the results of the pricing measure for the next year.

A standardized pricing process monitoring tool offers several advantages. First, it determines who is responsible for gathering which information to avoid gathering irrelevant or redundant information, which speeds up the process while ensuring the same accuracy of the information. Although the process is highly standardized, it is very flexible and can be abbreviated, for example, for tactical decisions that require less information than strategic decisions.

The new pricing process and its monitoring tool were implemented very quickly. The results of several pricing measures in the months following their implementation show that the pricing process of the bank was improved significantly and its goals were reached. Process standardization helped shorten the time for pricing decisions and allocated responsibilities to the process participants more efficiently. The integration of the sales department's view with the customer's view assured a high quality of the information and the resulting decisions.

Psychological aspects of pricing – odd prices versus even prices (private banking – cross product)

BACKGROUND AND GOALS

The reaction of customers to the price of a product or a service depends largely on how it is perceived. The knowledge of how important different price components are and how strongly they are perceived can be decisive for the success of pricing. The key questions are: what drives price awareness (do you know how much you are paying?) and price perception (is the price high or low?)? Which prices can be increased, which cannot? Are there certain psychological price thresholds beyond which customers drastically reduce their demand or are not willing to accept the price at all? These questions have important implications for price setting, price communication, marketing and sales.

In the consumer goods and retail industries, odd-prices, i.e. prices just below an even dollar or cents amount, such as €1.99 instead of €2.00, are widely deployed as a scheme of psychological price thresholds. Research in these industries teaches us that an odd-price, for example €9.90 is nearly judged as acceptable as €9, whereas €10 is much less accepted.

In the following case study, a major bank used these psychological aspects of pricing when exploring ways to raise its overall price levels. Its internal costs were rising due to tighter regulation and increased personnel costs, but the bank was afraid of losing customers to competitors if it increased prices too drastically or suddenly. The bank decided to search for an intelligent solution to increase prices, incorporating psychological aspects of pricing.

APPROACH AND KEY RESULTS

The first step of the analysis was to systematically determine the price-response functions and price elasticities for products with medium or high revenue contributions (for example, prices for checking accounts, deposit fees, transaction fees, interest rates). The approach for increasing prices must be differentiated based on the customers' perception of each price component. The approach for increasing prices for two price components in the securities business, the minimum price for a transaction and the annual deposit fee, was very different as these two price components are perceived in different ways.

While market research identified very low price awareness for the minimum price for a securities transaction, the price awareness of the deposit fee was very high. Customer research showed that the price elasticity for the minimum transaction fee was low; price changes cause a disproportionately small change in volume. Two out of three customers surveyed would not react at all when the minimum price for a transaction was raised from €25 to €30. Consequently, it was decided that this and other "hidden" price components could be increased in a simple, undifferentiated way without incorporating any additional price psychological aspects.

For the deposit fee, a more differentiated approach was necessary. Like the checking account fee and the mortgage interest rate, customers' price awareness for deposit fees was identified as being quite high. Together with a handful of other price components, these fees largely influenced the price image of the entire bank. A simple price increase would have led to major uproar by the customer base and, potentially, a loss of customers. The challenge was that the bank still aimed to increase its deposit fee and keep a favorable price image at the same time.

To achieve these two goals, information on possible price thresholds had to be gathered. With the help of the van Westendorp method, price response curves were determined and price thresholds were identified. For one segment, price thresholds were even slightly lower than the prices they were currently being charged. Findings from this exercise showed that while €19 was judged clearly favorable to €20 as one would expect, other prices were subject to this phenomenon as well. Somewhat surprisingly, €24 was also clearly favourable to €25. Based on these findings, the bank decided to set odd-prices for its annual deposit fee.

The same approach was applied to other price components. Some, like the annual deposit fee, were raised (from €15 to €19.90) to increase revenues, others were decreased to better attend to customer price thresholds and thus protect the bank's price image.

In summary, these differentiated price changes that incorporated information on price perception and price thresholds increased the bank's profit by a double-digit percentage and – as the market research results predicted – did not increase the churn rates significantly. Even better, the new, psychologically more attractive, price scheme was *perceived* as more attractive by both existing customers and new customers.

CONCLUSION

The psychological effects of pricing are becoming increasingly important for bank managers. The case study shown above is a good example of the intelligent use of information on price perception and price thresholds in the financial services sector. Banks that know how to gather this information and make use of it in their price setting processes can significantly increase their revenues while maintaining their positive price image.

Cross-products loyalty pricing scheme (retail/ private – cross product)

BACKGROUND AND GOALS

Within the last few years, the private banking market has become increasingly competitive. More and more players are entering the market as analysts predict attractive annual growth rates approaching 10 percent. Traditional private banks as well as independent asset managers are all trying to gain new customers and attract new money.

This case study shows how one of the key players in the market developed an innovative pricing scheme. Though it had several hundred billion Euro assets under management and more than 1 million individual customers worldwide, it was suffering from an increasingly tense market environment: the financial institution was experiencing net losses in customers as well as asset volume over of the course of a few years. Highly desirable customers, in particular, those who are either comparatively active (having a high number of transactions per annum) and/or possess a great amount of assets, left the bank for more attractive competitors. The bank consequently tried to explore options to regain these customers or at least to avoid further losses in these segments by introducing an intelligent loyalty pricing scheme.

APPROACH AND KEY RESULTS

Before the analysis performed by Simon-Kucher & Partners, the bank had a traditional customer recognition system: customers earning more than a certain threshold per month and having assets of more than €100,000 were awarded a "Gold" status, associated with additional services and reduced fees on selected banking products. While this system recognized large customers, it had some serious shortcomings. One issue was that those who once qualified for that bonus almost never lost it, even if they reduced their assets at the bank. Secondly, this system offered no incentive to customers who were not close to reaching the defined thresholds. Most importantly, the established system did not offer any "dynamic" elements that reward customers for their ongoing activity (number of transactions per year or annual asset growth).

In order to overcome these drawbacks, the financial institution designed a new cross-product loyalty pricing scheme. In workshops with marketing and sales managers, several design options (ways of earning and spending reward points) were developed. To assess the attractiveness of the various options, interviews with sales representatives and focus groups with costumers and non-customers were conducted. The economic effects of different design options were simulated based on the actual usage data of the customers. To enable this analysis, a sample of 30,000 customers was put into a database and a software tool calculated the effects of different program designs on new customers gained, new money managed and other variables. After several rounds of calculation and optimization, the new cross-product loyalty pricing scheme was established. It included a dynamic component that distributes bonus points to customers when the customer purchases investments, savings, insurance and other financial products, ensuring the program covered all relevant product areas. The higher a customer's transaction volume and annual growth of assets, the more points he or she earns. Thus, activity and asset concentration were both rewarded.

The collected bonus points could – as before – be redeemed for high value non-banking products, for example, necklaces or exclusive trips. More importantly, they could also be redeemed for price advantages on deposit and transaction fees or other benefits on savings products, retirement plans or investment funds.

IMPLEMENTATION AND CONCLUSION

The new loyalty program rewards active and growing customers. More than 80 percent of the customers who benefit from the new system are customers who belong to the target group of the financial institution. Even with highly pessimistic assumptions of the cost of technical implementation and administration of the new system, the level of customers' transaction and asset volumes yielded a positive profit effect very soon after the introduction of the program. A forecast shows that the break-even point could be reached only 4 years after the introduction of the new system.

The old customer recognition system offered no incentive scheme for investment and savings in general, nor any motivation for customers to maintain or grow their relationship with the bank. The new scheme addresses these shortfalls and sets clear incentives, and thus stimulates growth in new customers and assets. Due to its two-dimensional structure, it is attractive to different customer segments (active and growing), ensures that the goals of the customer and the bank are met, and, very importantly, is still very easy to understand for the consumer. From a financial perspective, the pay-off period of four years is acceptable, especially as the program is predicted to stimulate additional profits of more than €30 million in the first ten years after the introduction of the new system.

SEPA conforming payment packages

BACKGROUND AND GOALS

After the introduction of the Euro in 2002, one of the next steps to economic integration in Europe is the establishment of a Single European Payment Area (SEPA). The objective is to end the current isolation of domestic markets for electronic payments. After a transition phase (started in 2008) and final implementation, there will be no difference between domestic payments and payments between European countries. This means that all payment conditions and prices have to be aligned.

This also means that banks and transaction providers will be able to offer their services all over Europe. Even though the effect on retail customers is expected to be low, the impact on corporate customers will be significant:

- Corporate customers will need only one checking account from any bank in Europe to operate debit and credit transfers all over the continent.

- Multinational banks with large sales organizations will use this to win more corporate customers, taking advantage of the huge price differences across European countries (low price countries like Germany and the Netherlands, and high price countries like Spain and Italy).

- Large banks will also benefit from high processing volume creating excellent cost structures.

- This is also a chance for smaller banks, including Eastern European banks, to specialize and attack markets currently dominated by domestic players.

The current situation in most European countries, and especially in the relatively new member countries of Eastern Europe (for example, the Czech Republic, Poland, Slovenia) is characterized by vast price differences between national and international payment transactions. In these countries, often the biggest portion of banks' revenue from payment transactions is generated through (the relatively expensive) cross-border transactions while the national transactions are relatively inexpensive and consequently contribute only a small part to overall revenues (even although they are the majority in terms of transaction volume).

As all banks in the EU must have completely migrated to SEPA payments by 2010, many are currently rethinking their pricing for payment transactions. The bank in this case study is one of the largest banks of the new Eastern European EU countries with a special focus on payment transaction services for small and medium-sized companies, as well as for large domestic corporations. After the first countries of the region joined the EU, an increasing number of transactions became cross-border transactions to other EU countries ("Euro payments"). At the beginning of the project, prices for Euro payments were about ten times the price of domestic transactions, and the bank risked serious revenue losses if it simply lowered the price of Euro payments to the (much lower) national level. On the other hand, many of the bank's current customers used it only for transaction services; the penetration of other products, like business loans or business cards was very low. Consequently the goal of the project was not only to revise the bank's payment pricing, but to increase volumes and market share in product areas outside the core payment business as well.

APPROACH

Firstly, the strategic goals for the pricing of domestic transactions and Euro payments were set in workshops with senior management. These goals served as guidelines for the following step, which was to conduct a detailed revenue analysis of the payments business and the other product areas of the bank. This analysis delivered important insights regarding the profit potential of bundling different products together. Based on volume/revenue calculations, bundling options for an envisioned "Euro package" were identified. These options were then tested in discussions with the sales team as well as in focus groups with customers and non-customers of the bank's target segments (small/medium-sized companies and larger corporations). Both the sales interviews and the focus groups included workshop elements to determine price-response functions and price elasticities for the different bundling options. Overall, the qualitative and quantitative evaluations allowed the project team to select the optimal bundling structure and price ranges for a new bundled offering.

KEY RESULTS AND IMPLEMENTATION

Based on the analyses described above, the project delivered a detailed strategy and accompanying action plan for becoming SEPA compliant. The uptake rates of the package determined in the sales force interviews and customer focus groups were integrated in a business case. Although the bank lowered its prices for Euro payments drastically, the revenue losses were fully compensated by the package price for the Euro bundle and the revenues from the increased penetration of loans and business cards. In this way, the bank was able to turn the challenge SEPA into a strategic opportunity.

Price elasticity measurement for insurance businesses

BACKGROUND AND GOALS

Even after the insurer in this case study had undertaken cost reduction measures to improve its bottom line, it still faced poor combined ratios. Through extensive analysis, it was realized that price had the greatest potential for increasing profit, so management wanted to take the next step and exploit its full potential. However, implementing pricing measures confronted them with a typical dilemma; although an increase in price would lead to a higher profit margin, it was also clear that it would be offset by a reduction in contract volumes. Likewise, price reductions would increase contract volumes and simultaneously reduce margins. The key questions were: how strongly would customers react to price changes? What would be the combined impact of any price changes on volume and margin? Would all customers react in the same way? If not, how could those differences be leveraged by a differentiated and profit maximizing price strategy?

APPROACH

The first goal was to gain insight into the price elasticity of customers and then to understand if there were segments that shared the same elasticity. Previously the insurer had experimented with various pricing software packages which helped determine price elasticity. Unfortunately, these had failed to deliver satisfactory results. The price recommendations produced by the software "black-box" seemed somewhat contradictory for three reasons. First, they were based on historical internal data and could not take current competitive activities into account. Second, they were not able to distinguish whether a policy was terminated by a customer as a result of price change effects, or whether it was due to other factors. Third, the data did not allow them to project the effects of future actions at a granular level.

To reliably measure customer willingness-to-pay, a large scale customer research study using the conjoint measurement method was chosen. The trade-off decisions that the participants had to make on different products from different providers at different price levels helped determine their price elasticity.

Ideally, one would simply make a price adjustment to such a level that customers would not switch, keeping churn to a minimum. That rationale may have worked for the research sample, but it couldn't necessarily be applied to the rest of the customer base. Respondents were therefore clustered into different groups with the same (or nearly the same) price elasticity, and the elasticity information was mapped to the rest of the customer base. This was accomplished by analyzing correlations between information stored in the insurer's data warehouse and enriched by demographic data describing each segment.

A simulation model was developed in order to derive the optimal price adjustment for each segment. The model allowed the impact of price changes on volume and profit to be simultaneously calculated – for the entire existing book of business. In this way, the optimal price adjustment for each segment was determined.

The tool helped identify the profit maximizing price adjustment for different profit and churn rate scenarios. The tool also showed the improvement compared to a universal price adjustment across all customers.

To ensure full acceptance of the price adjustment by sales, the impact of the price adjustment on each sales agent's customer base was also analyzed. To reduce the potential burden on individual sales agents, price caps were introduced where disproportionally high churn rates were expected.

A period of discussion with the insurer's management about their market share and profit expectations was then held, and led to an optimal pricing strategy being developed based on the company's goals.

KEY RESULTS AND IMPLEMENTATION

The information on price elasticity allowed the insurer to fully leverage the potential of differentiated and customer-driven pricing and helped it to realize a much better result compared to undifferentiated, purely cost-driven price adjustments.

The tool made the effects on management goals, such as churn rates, market share and profit, fully transparent. For the first time, it allowed management to make fully informed decisions with a clear understanding of their expected impact.

Given the target additional churn of no more than 4 percent, as a result of the project, the insurer was able to increase profits by €21 million using a fully differentiated strategy. This differentiated approach represented an increase of 23 percent on current profits, and offered 50 percent more profit than the undifferentiated approach.

Successful product differentiation based on customer value in motor insurance

BACKGROUND AND GOALS

The insurer in this case study had a well established business in the motor insurance market. Its goal was to be premium-oriented, but at the same time, to be a mass insurer. The insurer tackled the market with a multi-brand strategy comprised of various motor insurance brands in the market. The products from each brand were nearly identical in their cover and cover levels. Typically, they were developed centrally and from a purely internal perspective. Product and actuarial experts, and to an extent the sales team, generated ideas which were simply implemented based on cost and margin calculations.

Due to the typical motor insurance price cycle, the risk of premium and profit erosion had recently risen sharply. The insurer was also affected by a softening market. Projections for premium income for the upcoming year were based on a reduction of up to 4 percent, on average, across the entire customer base, and implied a significant reduction in new business premiums.

Moreover, each year the general price pressure was intensified by a fourth quarter price war in which nearly all motor insurers regularly participated. As all policies expired with the calendar year, each insurer tried to gain market share by winning over competitors' customers. Needless to say, their main argument in motivating customers to switch providers was lower prices. As a consequence, every year the insurer's share of price sensitive customers was naturally increasing, and led to a widely accepted belief that motor insurance had become a commodity and that price was the only relevant decision criteria. Reality presented a different picture. The market was still highly intransparent to customers, with over 100 providers/brands in the market, of which the top ten brands did not even account for 50 percent of total premium generated. Price differences of several hundred basis points among brands were common. The majority of customers were loyal to their providers, but a growing low price segment and new providers selling over the Internet meant that the overall market had become more differentiated and heterogeneous.

In this environment, the insurer searched for new ways to stabilize its current premium volume and profits, or even to slightly grow them relative to the market. The project's goals were to extract revenue and profit potential...

- ...from current and potentially new customers...

- ...with an optimized product and pricing approach...

- ...that not only considers the internal perspective, but is mainly based on customers' product preferences and their willingness-to-pay.

APPROACH

The first step focused on generating potential ideas to generate extra premium volume. For this exercise, a wide range of information sources was tapped. Sales, as well as internal product, market and actuarial experts, all provided input. Also, a national and international benchmarking analysis was conducted to enrich the internal information gathered with external sources. The data was then presented and discussed in focus groups with current and potential customers. This helped to filter and prioritize the unstructured information from a customer perspective.

In step 2, the task was to understand the level of importance customers place on the current as well as potential product features. For this, a short customer research in the form of KANO analysis was conducted that classified current and potential product features into "musts", "attractives" and "indifferents". The analysis was based on the following lines of inquiry: what do customers perceive as absolute must haves, causing dissatisfaction when missing in a policy? What do customers perceive as attractive features, leading to satisfaction and willingness-to-pay? Were there any product features that could be eliminated since they did not generate value to customers and only contributed to cost? This was the input for step 3.

The findings from the KANO analysis were validated on a larger basis, but, more importantly, customer preferences for each product feature were measured, and simultaneously their willingness-to-pay was gathered. As the preference structure turned out to be fairly heterogeneous, a segmentation analysis was conducted to learn more about how (potential) customers differed in their preferences. Three different segments were identified among both the insurer's current book and target customers, including a price-driven segment, primarily interested in an inexpensive product; a reward-oriented segment, seeking monetary recognition through a bonus system; and a value-segment searching for comprehensive coverage.

The segment information was then transferred from the research sample to the entire customer database. For this, a rule was developed that described the sample segments with data available in an internal data warehouse. The rule made it easy to assign each existing customer to one of the three preference segments.

A custom simulation model was then developed that not only helped simulate profit-optimal product designs per segment, but optimized products when all customer groups were considered together. These outcomes were then discussed and refined together with the sales, product and actuarial teams, thus fostering broad internal acceptance.

KEY RESULTS AND IMPLEMENTATION

The project helped the insurer change its internally driven approach to one that included the customer perspective in its product strategy and pricing decisions.

The new approach highlighted that the current practice of "one size fits all" product and pricing was not at all suitable. The market was differentiated, and in order to reduce churn and avoid the need to offer vast discounts, the market needed to be served in a differentiated manner. The preference segments identified could not only be found in this brand, but also in the customer bases of the insurer's different brands. As a consequence, the differentiation strategy could be implemented consistently across all its brands.

In the end, the current product was divided into two products. A lean but cheap product targeted purely price-driven customers. All product features not perceived as absolute musts were removed from the policy. This gave room for price decreases of up to 4 percent compared to current products. The second product, a value product, offered new and highly valued product features. This generated an additional willingness-to-pay of 8 percent with the value-driven customers. In addition to these base products, an optional module was developed. It contained bonus elements and was designed with the reward-driven customers in mind.

With this differentiated and customer value driven product portfolio, the insurer had the potential not only to stabilize its market position, but also to increase profits by 8 percent. With combined ratios close to 100 percent, this represents a significant improvement.

The success of the project can also be attributed to the fact that using the segment classification rule, marketing and sales teams were able to systematically contact and upgrade all value driven customers to the new product. Another tool for new customers asked five questions in the course of a sales discussion to classify every prospect into one of the three segments, and thus make a targeted product offering possible.

Insights for Financial Services Managers

The following theses provide a summary of the book's most important lessons:

1. **Thesis 1:** the importance of pricing in financial services institutions is increasing with the price pressure in the industry. Pricing must be managed more professionally.

2. **Thesis 2:** competing on price alone is dangerous. Mistakes in managing prices can destroy margins. To avoid price wars, professional price management methods must be employed.

3. **Thesis 3:** financial services managers must fully understand that price is the number one driver of profit in the modern competitive landscape. To determine the optimal price, price-response functions must be known and information on customers' willingness-to-pay and price elasticities must be collected.

4. **Thesis 4:** multiple methods to derive this important information and to calculate price-response functions are available. Which method to choose (e.g. expert judgment, direct customer survey, indirect techniques like conjoint measurement) depends on the specific case at hand.

5. **Thesis 5:** a number of issues should be considered when calculating the price-response functions of financial services products. Most importantly, the product or service at hand must be precisely defined for the customer so that he is able to make educated trade-off decisions. Secondly, when measuring price elasticity and willingness-to-pay, the customer's decision process must be recreated as realistically as possible.

6. **Thesis 6:** many financial services institutions are in need of new pricing processes to optimize their pricing decisions. To improve the entire decision making process significantly, information and

knowledge of pricing issues should be thoroughly distributed throughout the organization.

7.   **Thesis 7:** clear strategic pricing goals and pricing guidelines are the foundation of an effective pricing process. They should be developed and clearly communicated by senior management, and incentive systems should be realigned to these new goals.

8.   **Thesis 8:** smart product and price differentiation can significantly increase profitability. Innovative forms like non-linear pricing, price bundling or multi-person pricing should be explored in more detail and introduced in as many areas as possible.

9.   **Thesis 9:** the extent to which a price change impacts sales, revenue and profit depends on how a price is perceived by customers. Hence, psychological aspects of pricing should be considered more often in the pricing of products. Financial services institutions often lack information on customers' price perception, and price thresholds are often neglected. Profits are being left on the table.

10.   **Thesis 10:** price management is often insufficiently supported by the organizational structure of financial services institutions. The roles of the organizational entities involved in the pricing process have to be defined more clearly. Other industries, like automotive and pharmaceuticals, are good benchmarks for improving organizational structures when it comes to pricing.

11.   **Thesis 11:** in almost any financial services institution a huge amount of information remains untouched and hidden in extensive IT systems. This information is a significant source that can help build "pricing intelligence" in the organization (e.g. through structured pricing databases, pricing information systems and pricing reports) and should be tapped more systematically.

12.   **Thesis 12:** developing intelligent pricing concepts is important, but the critical step is implementing pricing well. The delegation of pricing responsibilities within an organization must be aligned with the company's competitive situation and corporate strategy. Clear discount allowance structures and incentive systems must be developed and implemented in the market to ensure an optimal enforcement of prices.

Index

If you have found this book useful you may be interested in other titles from Gower

Accounting Irregularities in Financial Statements:
A Definitive Guide for Litigators, Auditors and Fraud
Investigators
Benny Kwok
978-0-566-08621-2

Commercial Due Diligence:
The Key to Understanding Value in an Acquisition
Peter Howson
978-0-566-08651-9

Competitive Intelligence:
Gathering, Analysing and Putting it to Work
Christopher Murphy
978-0-566-08537-6

Countering Terrorist Finance:
A Training Handbook for Financial Services
Tim Parkman and Gill Peeling
978-0-566-08725-7

Data Protection in the Financial Services Industry
Mandy Webster
978-0-566-08662-5

Developing and Managing a Successful Payment Cards
Business
Jeff Slawsky and Samee Zafar
978-0-566-08648-9

GOWER